SUPPORTING YOU THROUGH EVERY STAGE

STAGE 1
WORKBOOK

A study and revision aid for the BHS Stage 1 assessment

KENILWORTH PRESS

First published in the UK in 2008 by Kenilworth Press
an imprint of Quiller Publishing Ltd

Reprinted 2010, 2012, 2014, 2015, 2017

This new edition published 2018

© The British Horse Society 2008

All rights reserved. No part of this publication may be reproduced, stored in a retrieval system, or transmitted in any form or by any means, electronic, mechanical, photocopying, recording or otherwise, without the written permission of the copyright holder.

British Library Cataloguing in Publication Data
A catalogue record for this book is available from the British Library

ISBN 978 1 910016 32 9

Layout and illustrations by Carole Vincer
Revisions by Arabella Ainslie
Jacket cover by Howard Taylor

Printed in China

Appointed GPSR EU Representative: Easy Access System Europe Oü, 16879218
Address: Mustamäe tee 50, 10621, Tallinn, Estonia
Contact Details: gpsr.requests@easproject.com, +358 40 500 3575

KENILWORTH PRESS
An imprint of Quiller Publishing Ltd
The Hill, Merrywalks, Stroud
Gloucestershire, GL5 4EP
Tel: 01453 847800
Email: info@quillerbooks.com
Website: www.quillerpublishing.com

DISCLAIMER: The authors and publishers shall have neither liability nor responsibility to any person or entity with respect to any loss or damage caused or alleged to be caused directly or indirectly by the information contained in this book. While the book is as accurate as the authors can make it, there may be errors, omissions, and inaccuracies.

CONTENTS

Introduction 4

QUESTIONS
1. Grooming 5
2. Rugs 9
3. Saddlery 14
4. Handling 22
5. Maintaining Clean Stables 24
6. The Foot and Shoeing 28
7. Anatomy and Handling 32
8. Health and Safety 39
9. Horse Health 43
10. Horse Behaviour 48
11. Basic Grassland Care 54
12. Watering and Feeding 60
13. General Knowledge 66
14. Riding 68

ANSWERS 80

Further Reading 108
Useful Addresses 108

INTRODUCTION

This workbook has been compiled as a revision aid for candidates preparing for the BHS Stage 1 assessment. It is designed to be used in conjunction with a Stage 1 course, ideally provided by a BHS Approved Training Centre, where coaches have a good understanding of the BHS Equine Excellence Pathway.

The questions have been written to captivate the imagination and help to make revision and quizzing of knowledge entertaining, whilst maintaining the integrity and quality of the assessment for which the student is preparing.

The authors wish to stress that there is no 'BHS way' for either practical or theory. As such there may be more answers to questions than have been given. The BHS system aims to train practical, safe and efficient horsemen and women, thus providing a foundation of internationally recognised qualifications from which a person may develop in any equestrian direction.

Details of further reading and contact details for the BHS are given at the end of the book.

BHS revision workbooks are available for Stage 1 and Stage 2

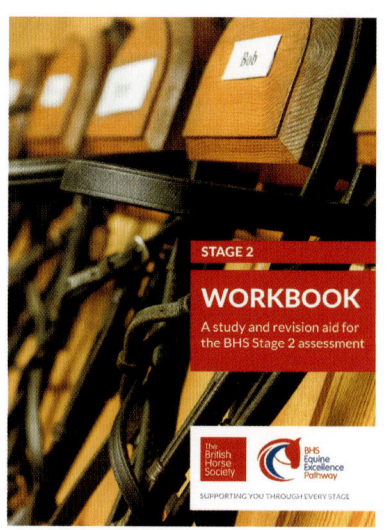

1 GROOMING

Q1.1 Identify and describe the purpose of each of these grooming kit items.

A		
B		
C		
D		
E		
F		
G		
H		
I		
J		
K		

1 GROOMING

Q1.2 Below is a list of reasons for grooming. Explain each.

Health

Condition

Prevention of disease

Appearance

Checking for new heat/swelling

Cleanliness

Q1.3 Put the grooming sequence in the correct order for brushing off when the horse is wearing a rug. (1–10)

Quartering

- [ ] • Undo and secure the rug fastenings
- [ ] • Tie up the horse
- [ ] • Fold the front of the rug back
- [ ] • Fold the rear of the rug forward
- [ ] • Sponge eyes, nose and dock
- [ ] • Pick out the feet
- [ ] • Brush the front of the body and mane
- [ ] • Clean the tail
- [ ] • Secure the rug
- [ ] • Brush the back of the horse

Q1.4 Why is it important to be efficient when grooming?

_____

_____

_____

1 GROOMING

Q1.5 Grooming — can you spot eight unsafe practices in this picture? List them in the space below.

1. _____

2. _____

3. _____

4. _____

5. _____

6. _____

7. _____

8. _____

2 RUGS

Q2.1 State the uses for each type of rug.

LIGHTWEIGHT TURNOUT RUG WITH NO NECK COVER

MIDDLEWEIGHT TURNOUT RUG WITH A DETACHABLE NECK COVER

FULL NECK HEAVYWEIGHT TURNOUT RUG

SUMMER SHEET

COOLER RUG

FLEECE

LIGHTWEIGHT STABLE RUG

HEAVYWEIGHT STABLE RUG

FLY RUG

2 RUGS

Q2.2 Match the sentences to the pictures to describe how to put on a rug.

1. Securely tie up the horse.
2. Place the rug over the horse's withers.
3. Fasten the front strap.
4. Unfold the rug.
5. Secure the middle straps, crossing them underneath the horse's stomach.
6. Fasten the leg straps/pull the tail over the fillet string.

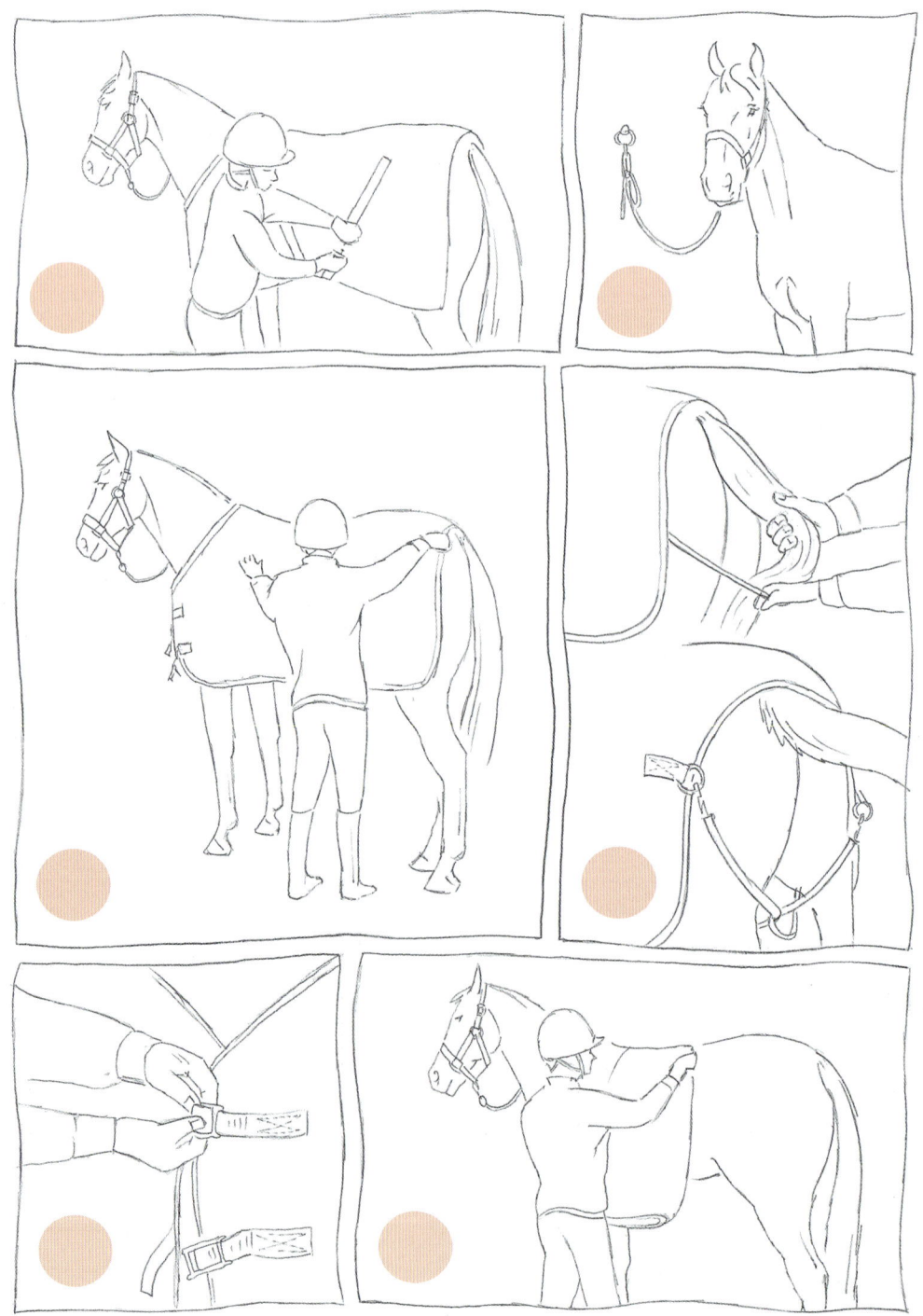

Q2.3 Label and describe the areas of good fit on the rug below.

Q2.4 Label and describe the areas of poor fit on the rug below.

2 RUGS

Q2.5 Number these images in the correct sequence to show how to fasten leg straps. Two of the images are incorrect — can you spot them?

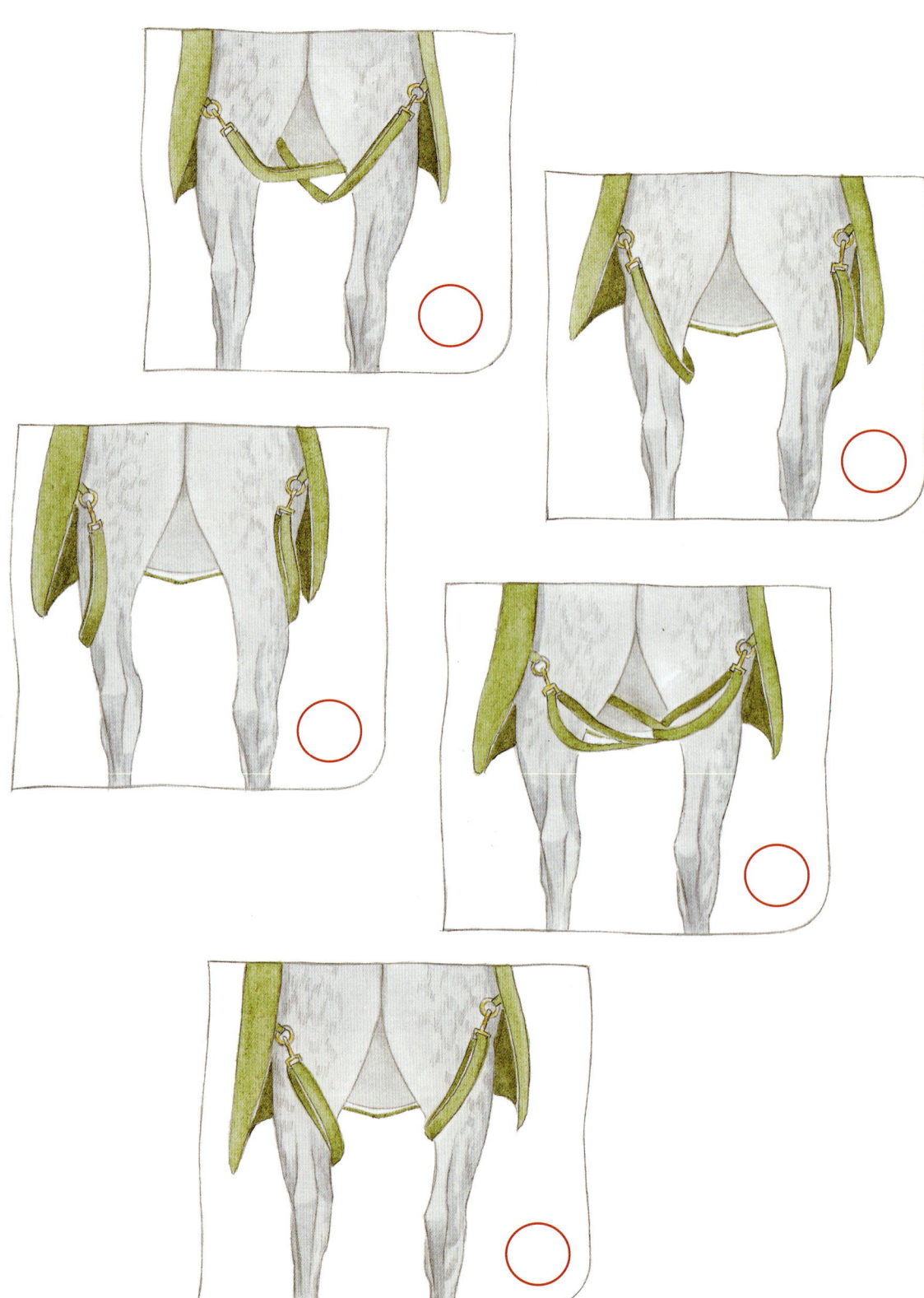

12

2 RUGS

Q2.6 Consider whether the following statements describing the correct, safe method to remove a rug are true or false. Tick the appropriate boxes.

STATEMENT	True	False
The horse should be securely tied, using a headcollar and quick-release knot.		
The fastenings can be undone in any order as long as a safe procedure is followed.		
The rug is folded front half over back half, and then slid back over the horse's hindquarters and removed.		
The fastenings are tied up before removal to prevent them hitting the horse.		

Q2.7 These jumbled descriptions refer to stable rugs, turnout rugs and coolers. Can you work out which is which and write them in the chart below? (Some apply to more than one type of rug.)

- Some have tail flaps
- Durable
- Non-waterproof
- Duvet-like filling
- Usually has leg straps
- Maintains warmth whilst allowing the horse to cool down
- Tough
- Wicks away moisture from the horse
- Usually has a fillet string
- Waterproof

STABLE	TURNOUT	COOLER

3 SADDLERY

Q3.1 Label as many parts of the saddle as you can.

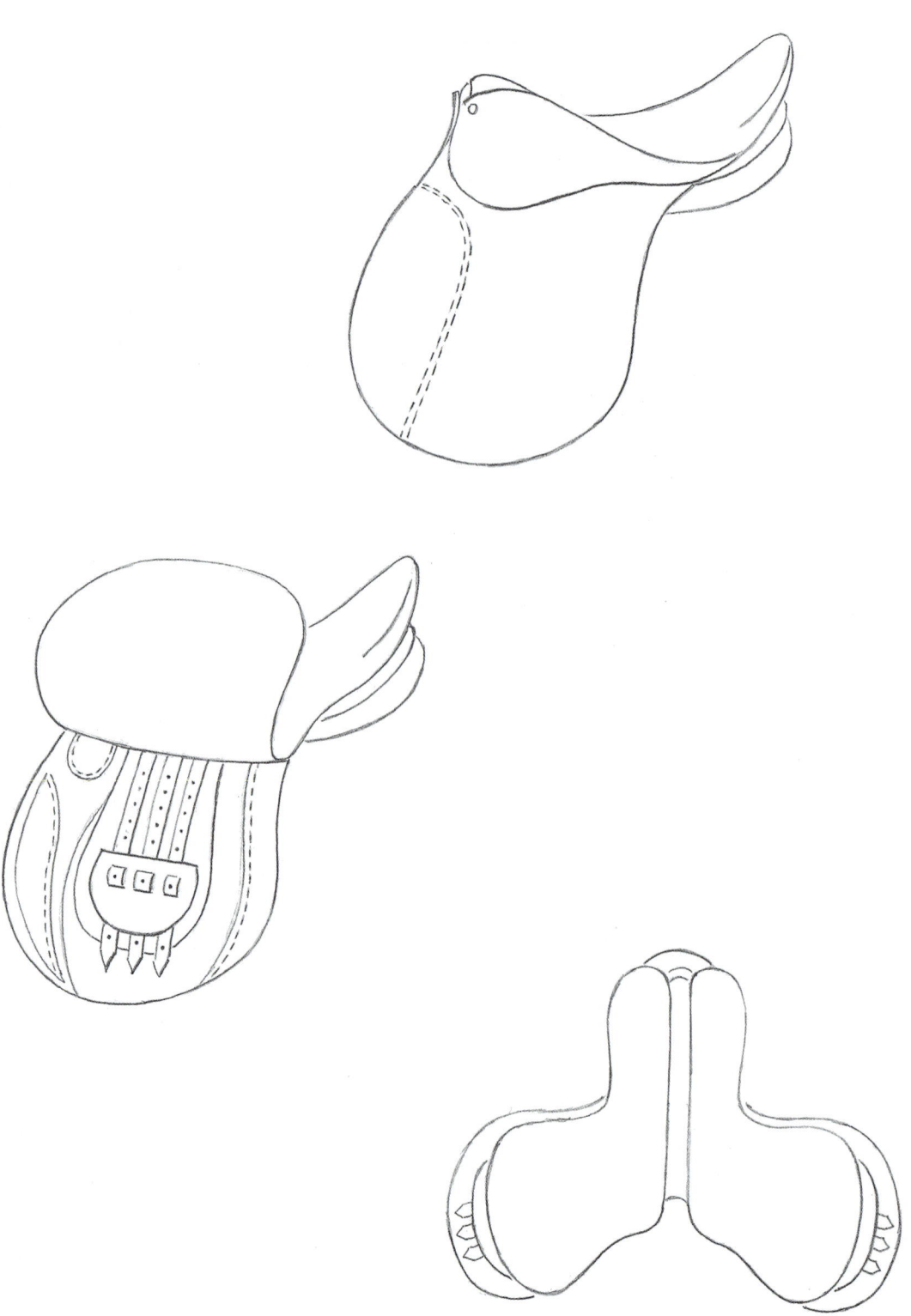

Q3.2 Label the parts of the bridle.

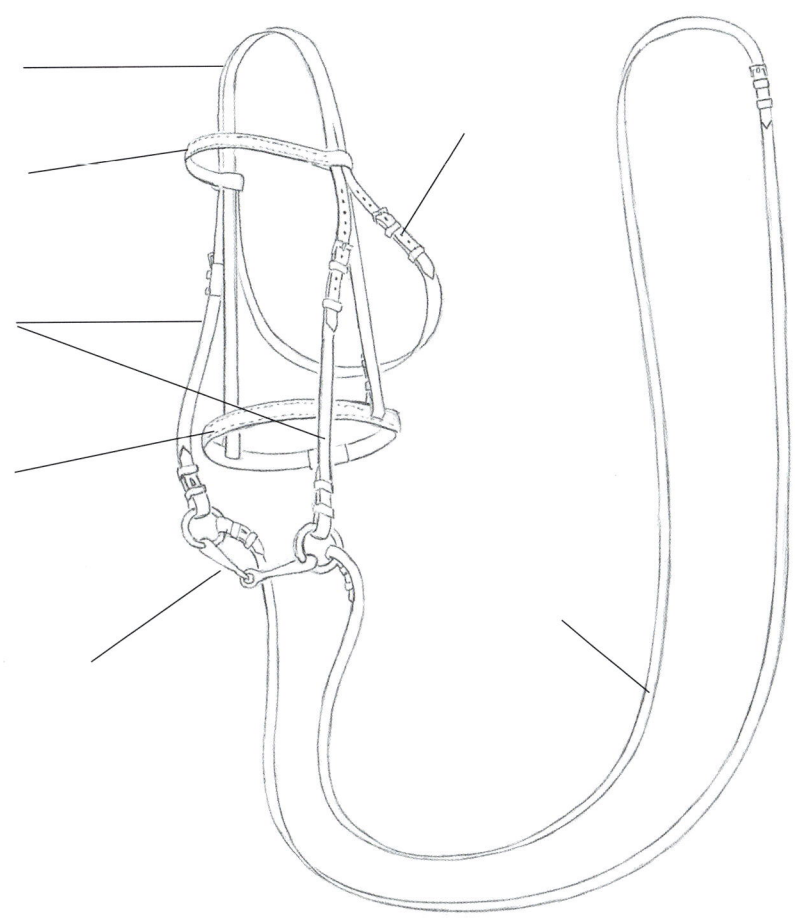

Q3.3 When putting on a saddle, what should you check to ensure the horse's comfort? List as many points as you can.

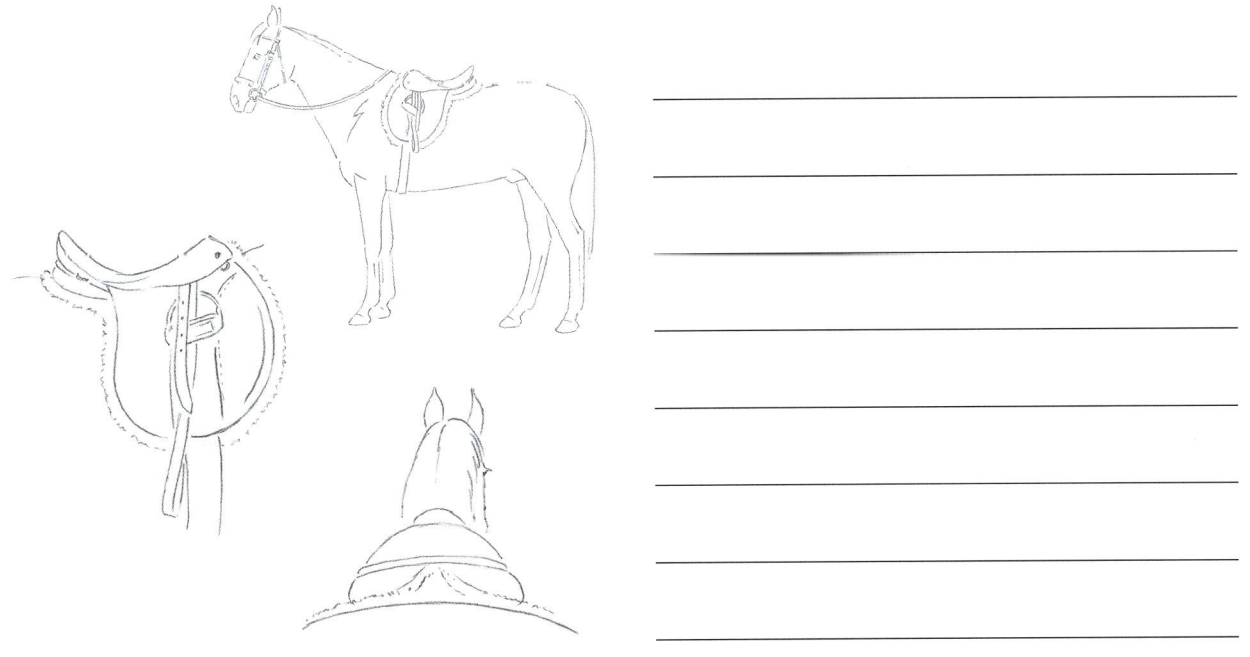

3 SADDLERY

Q3.4 Look at these drawings of a running and a standing martingale. Describe how to check the fit of each martingale correctly.

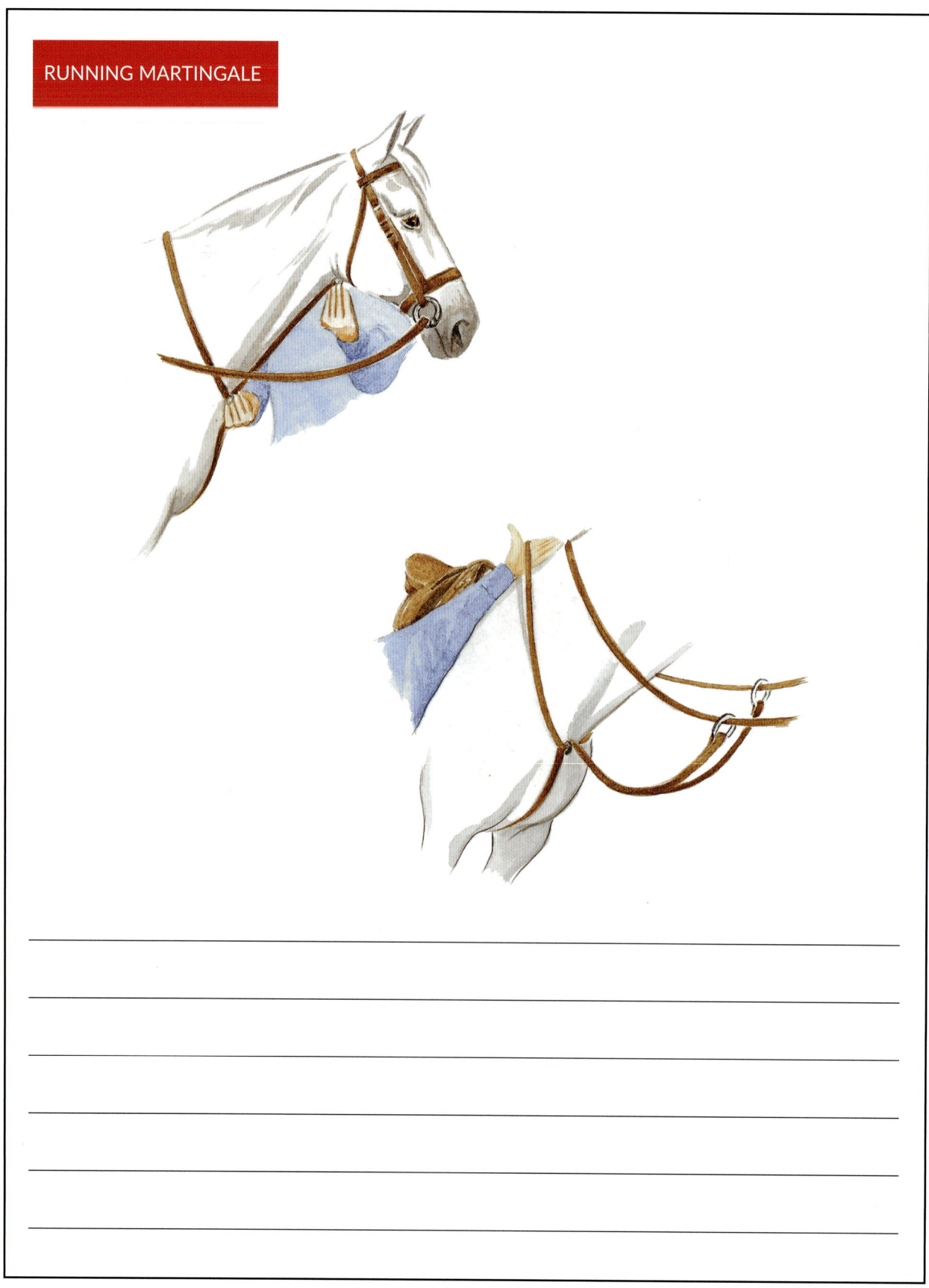

STANDING MARTINGALE

_____
_____
_____
_____
_____
_____
_____

Q3.5 Complete the table by describing the potential consequences of using dirty or worn tack.

DIRTY GIRTH	
THIN STIRRUP LEATHERS	
WORN STITCHING ON STIRRUP LEATHERS	
DIRTY NUMNAH	
WORN STITCHES ON GIRTH STRAPS	

3 SADDLERY

Q3.6 Tacking up. Number the pictures from 1–10, putting them into sequence and describe the correct tacking-up procedure at each stage.

1 _____
2 _____
3 _____
4 _____
5 _____
6 _____
7 _____
8 _____
9 _____
10 _____

18

Q3.7 Untacking. Number the pictures from 1–10, putting them into sequence, and describe the correct untacking procedure at each stage.

1 _____
2 _____
3 _____
4 _____
5 _____
6 _____
7 _____
8 _____
9 _____
10 _____

3 SADDLERY

Q3.8 (a) In what sizes are numnahs produced?
(b) Fill in the gaps, using the words provided, to describe how to fit a numnah.

(a) _____

> forward   gullet   loops   numnah   saddle   hair

(b) Place the _____ on the horse's back a little further _____ than the position of the the saddle. Place the _____ on top and pull the numnah up into the _____ of the saddle. Slide both saddle and numnah back into the correct position; this aids the _____ to lie flat. Attach the numnah to the saddle by the _____ usually positioned for the girth.

Q3.9 Name the types of noseband shown below. Describe how they fasten and their action.

_____

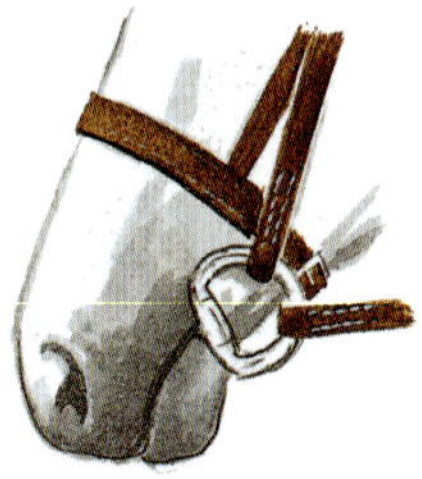

_____

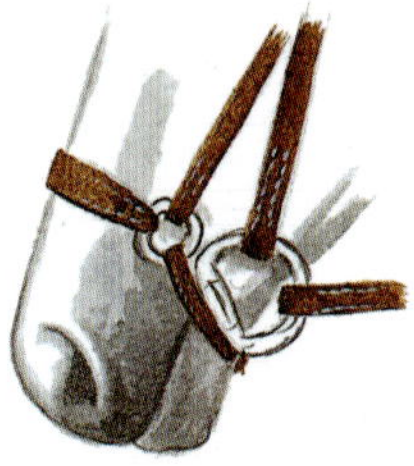

_____

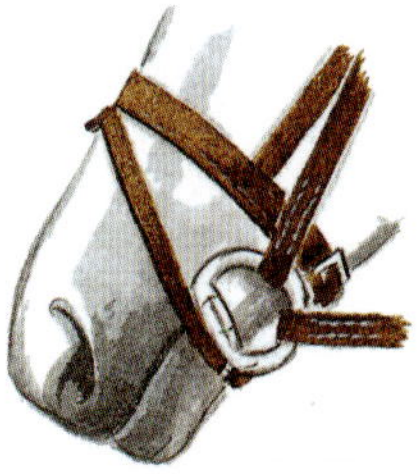

20

Q3.10 (a) Explain the purpose of each stage of tack cleaning.
(b) What is the reason for 'stripping' tack?

(a) _____

(b) _____

4 HANDLING

Q4.1 Below is a yard scene filled with hazards. Circle the areas of potential danger to horse and people.

Q4.2 Explain the following principles of handling and working with horses.

SAFETY

RISK ASSESSMENTS

RESPECT BETWEEN HORSE AND GROOM

COMMUNICATION

DISCIPLINE

ROUTINE

4 HANDLING

Q4.3 Using the words provided, fill in the gaps to explain how to put on and fit a headcollar.

> shoulder   poll   lead rope   two fingers'   head   noseband

Prepare the headcollar ready for use by unravelling the _____ if rolled, ensuring that the _____ is done up and that the headpiece is undone. Approach the horse at his _____. Standing just in front of the shoulder, facing the horse's _____, lift the noseband over the nose. Position the headpiece over the _____, avoiding the ears and fasten the buckle. To check the fit, the noseband should have _____ width below the projecting cheek bone and two fingers' width between the noseband and the face.

Q4.4 (a) List three basic safety checks that you might make before being happy to tie up a horse in an unknown environment.
(b) Number these images of tying a quick-release knot in the correct sequence.

(a) _____

_____

(b)

Q4.5 Why is it important to use time efficiently, as well as being safe, when working with horses?

_____

_____

_____

_____

5 MAINTAINING CLEAN STABLES

Q5.1 Fill in the gaps in the table with appropriate comments on the various types of bedding.

BEDDING	STRAW	SHAVINGS	HEMP	PAPER	RUBBER MATTING
EXPENSIVE	Depends on season				Initial cost
EDIBLE					No
EASY STORAGE				Yes	
EASY DISPOSAL			Yes		
DUSTY					No
COMFORT					
CLEAN					Always use with bedding

Q5.2 List four reasons why we use bedding.

1. _____

2. _____

3. _____

4. _____

5 MAINTAINING CLEAN STABLES

Q5.3 Fill in the gaps to make sense of the paragraph describing mucking out.

| mucked out | draughts | bedding | thinner | lie down | bedding | skipped out |

Although types of _____ vary, maintenance is fairly similar. They are generally _____ daily and _____ every time you enter the stable. Day beds tend to be _____ , with the bedding thrown up into the banks. More _____ may be added to night beds so that the horse has a thicker bed in which to _____ at night. Banks are built to stop _____ and to prevent the horse from becoming cast.

Q5.4 List the advantages and disadvantages of daily mucking out and deep littering.

ADVANTAGES	DISADVANTAGES
DAILY MUCKING OUT	
DEEP LITTERING	

5 MAINTAINING CLEAN STABLES

Q5.5 Mucking out. Put the list below into the correct order from 1–8 to explain the correct procedure.

- [ ] Lay the bed.
- [ ] Remove the water buckets.
- [ ] Throw all the bedding up one or two banks (rotated daily).
- [ ] Remove the horse from the stable or tie up securely.
- [ ] Sweep the floor.
- [ ] Remove the wet area.
- [ ] Replace the freshly filled water buckets.
- [ ] Remove the droppings.

Q5.6 Describe how to skip out and tidy a stable.

_____
_____
_____
_____

Q5.7 Describe how to maintain a muck heap that has three separate heaps.

_____
_____
_____
_____
_____

5 MAINTAINING CLEAN STABLES

Q5.8 Below is a picture of a stable being incorrectly mucked out. List the four mistakes being made.

1. _____

2. _____

3. _____

4. _____

6 THE FOOT AND SHOEING

Q6.1 Picking out the feet. Describe what is happening in each picture.

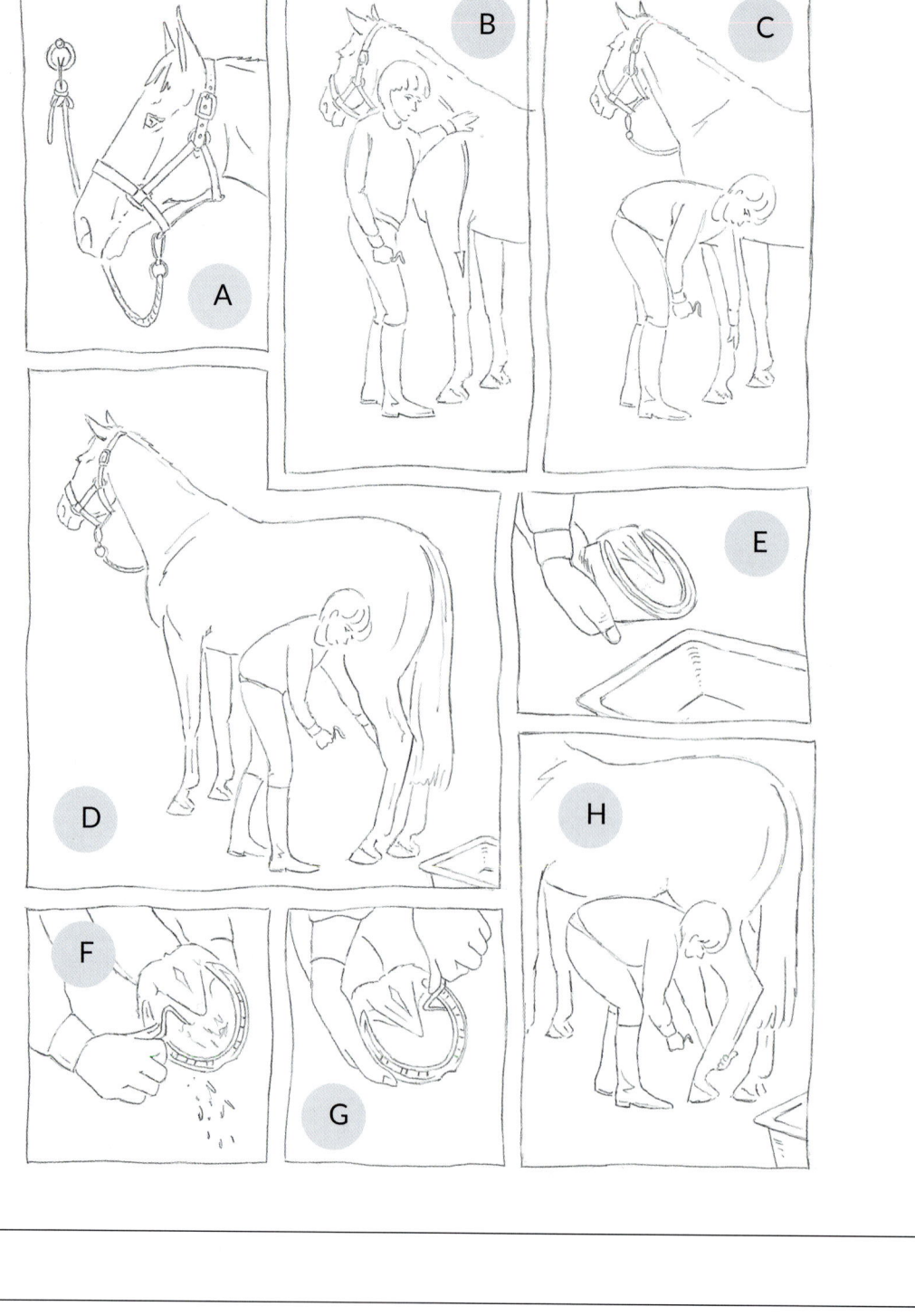

A _____

B _____

C _____

D _____

E _____

F _____

G _____

H _____

Q6.2 Fill in the gaps, using the words provided, to explain how to wash and oil the horse's feet.

> oil   water   hooves   scrub   dressing

Using a _____ brush, clean the outside of the _____. Pick up each foot in turn and gently _____ the underside of each hoof. Once the feet are dry, oil inside and out using hoof _____ or _____.

Q6.3 Match these shoeing terms to their correct definitions.

Term	Meaning	Term
Recently shod	thin, wafer-like shoes that may actually snap	
In need of shoeing	the shoe has come off	
Risen clenches	shod one or two weeks ago	
Twisted shoe	as the toe grows, it takes the shoe forward causing the clenches to rise	
Loose shoe	the shoe is not flat on the horse's foot; it may be pulled away from the foot and be bent	
Cast shoe	many horses grow more at the toe than at the heel and therefore give the impression of long toes	
Worn thin	growth over the sides of the shoe	
Long feet	the foot requires attention	
Overgrown foot	movement of the shoe when examined	

6 THE FOOT AND SHOEING

Q6.4 Label as many external parts of the foot as you can.

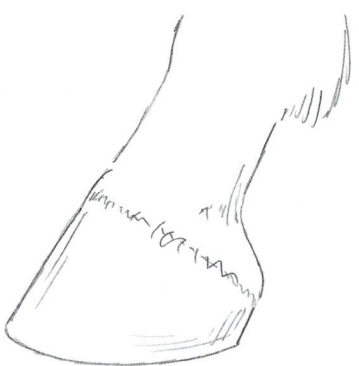

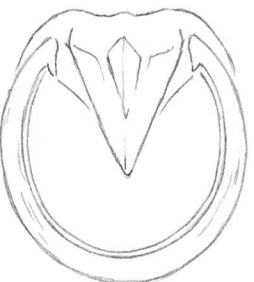

Q6.5 Label these diagrams to show the key points of a well-shod foot.

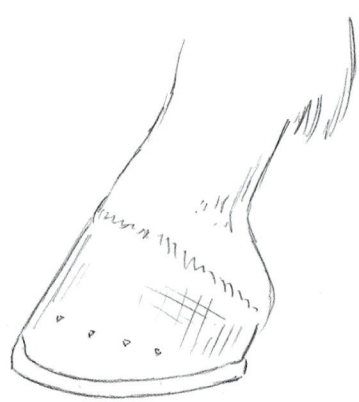

6 THE FOOT AND SHOEING

Q6.6 This foot is in need of shoeing. Can you label the tell-tale signs?

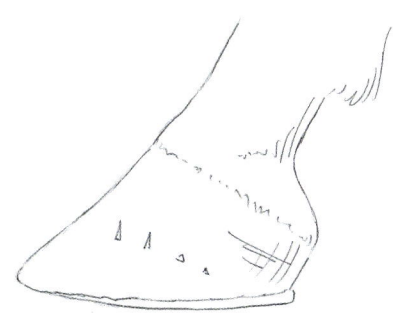

7 ANATOMY AND HANDLING

Q7.1 Label the points of a horse.

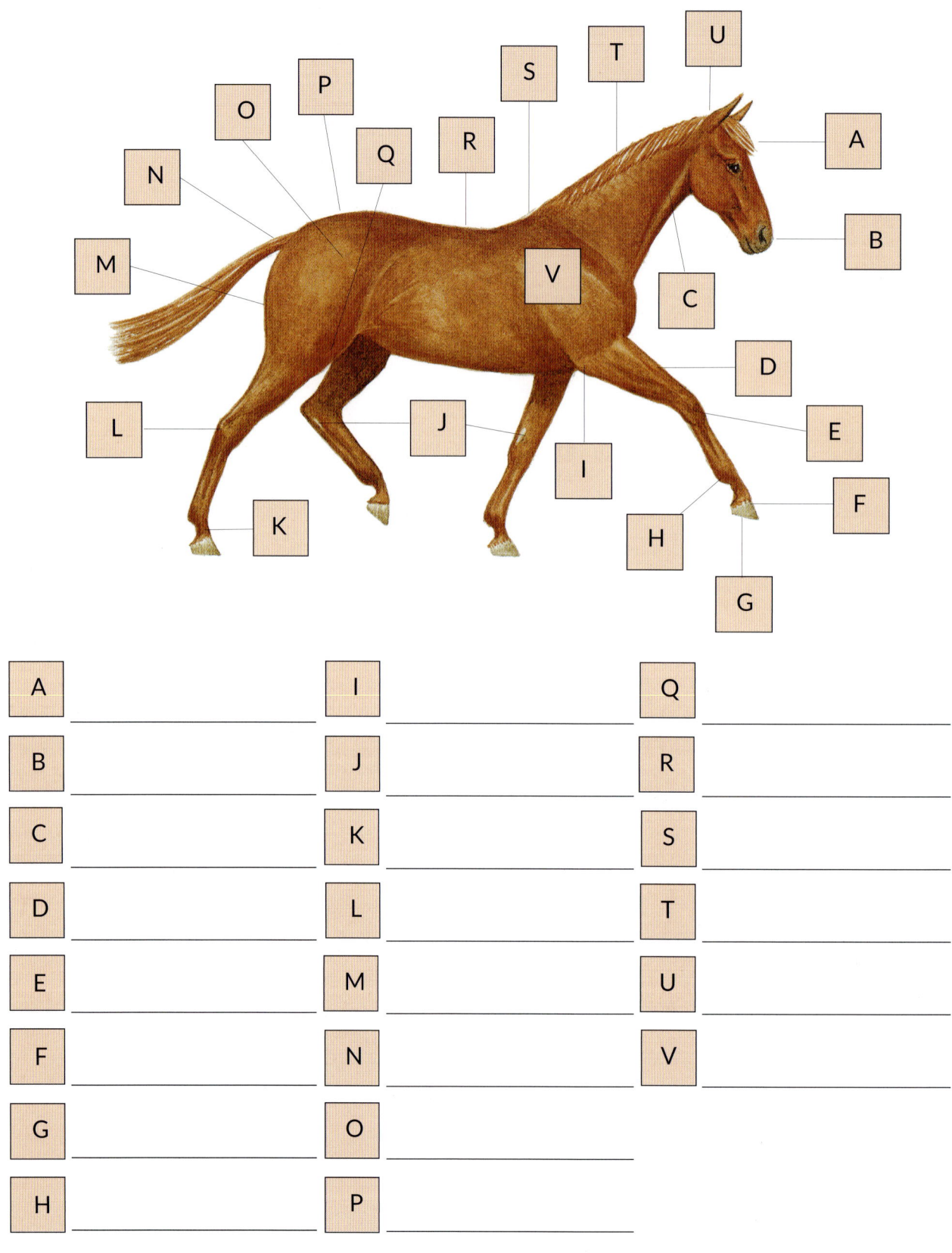

A _____
B _____
C _____
D _____
E _____
F _____
G _____
H _____

I _____
J _____
K _____
L _____
M _____
N _____
O _____
P _____

Q _____
R _____
S _____
T _____
U _____
V _____

7 ANATOMY AND HANDLING

Q7.2 Describe each of these horse colours.

BAY	
GREY	
CHESTNUT	
BLACK	
BROWN	
DUN	
PALOMINO	
PIEBALD	
SKEWBALD	
SPOTTED	
ROAN	

7 ANATOMY AND HANDLING

Q7.3 There are further terms to describe greys and spotted horses. Label each picture.

GREY

SPOTTED

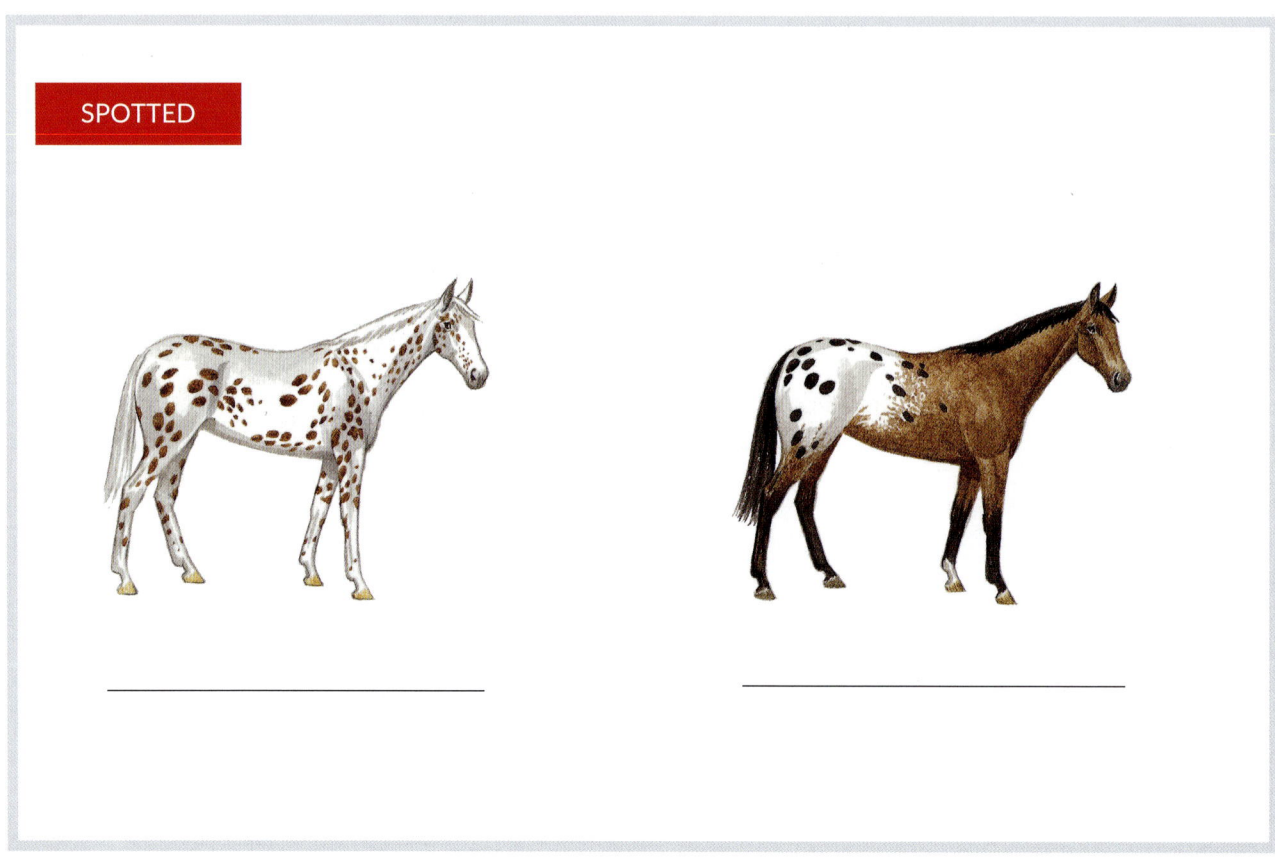

7 ANATOMY AND HANDLING

Q7.4 Name each of these facial markings.

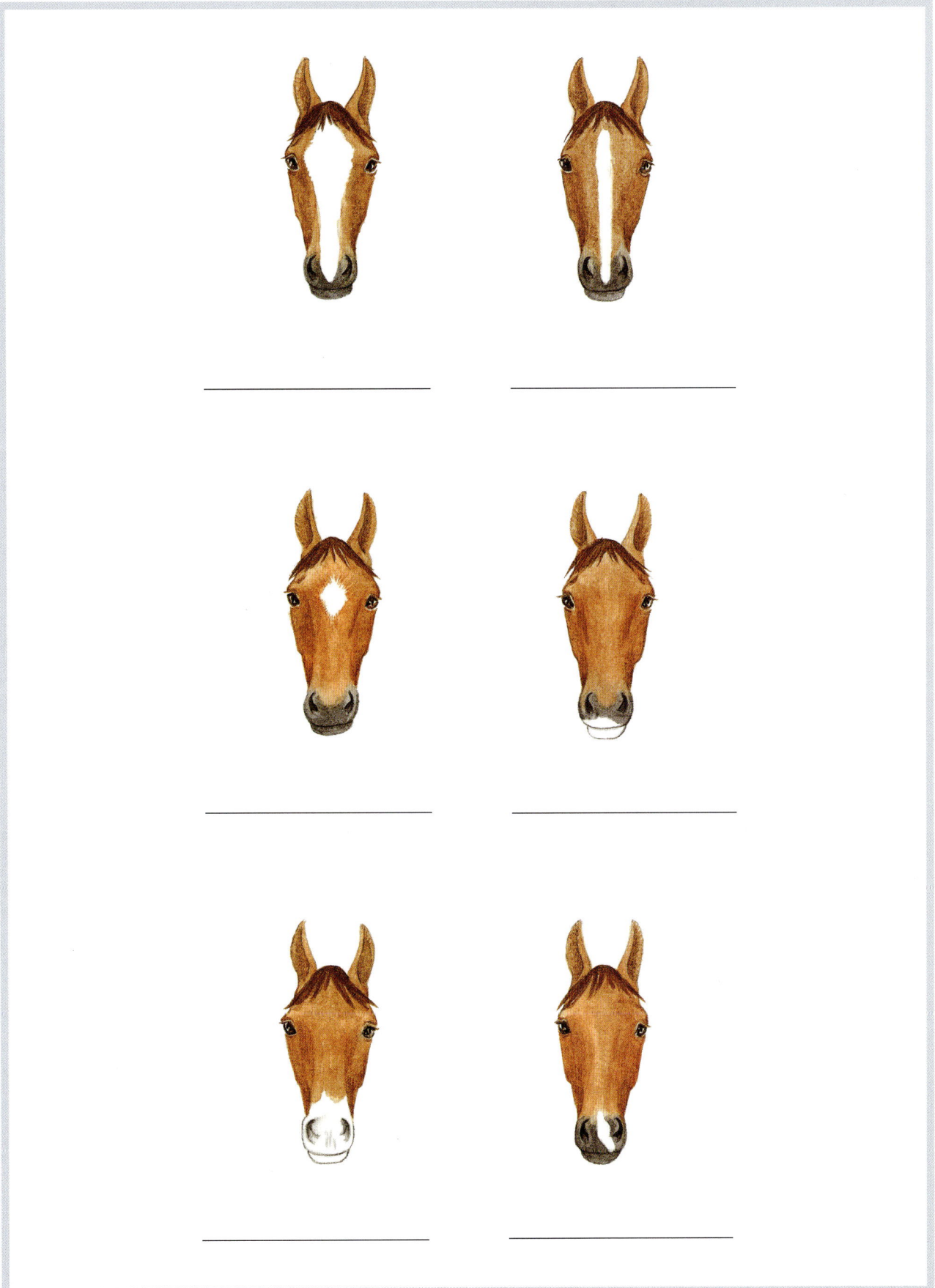

7 ANATOMY AND HANDLING

Q7.5 Colour in each blank leg to show the markings named below.

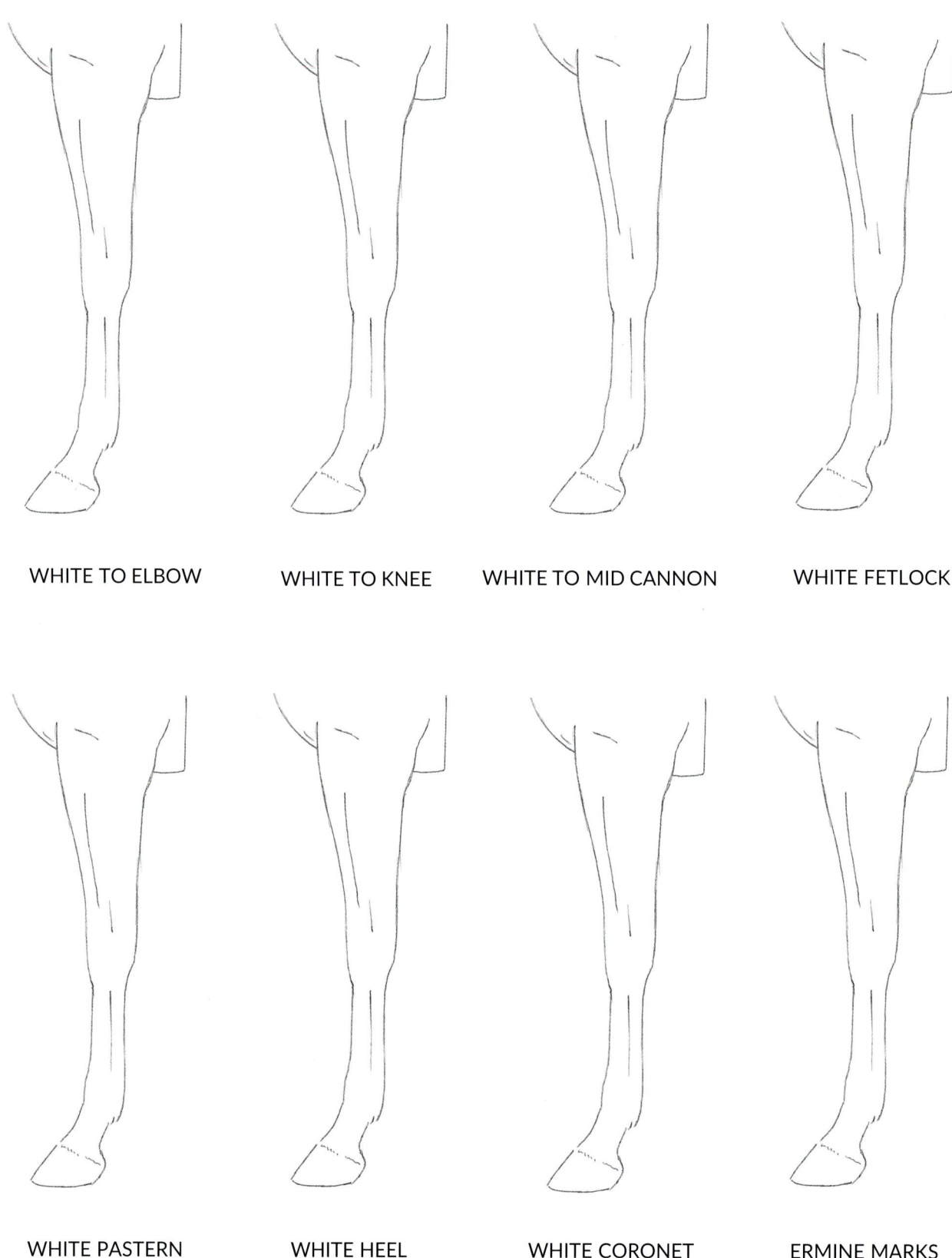

WHITE TO ELBOW WHITE TO KNEE WHITE TO MID CANNON WHITE FETLOCK

WHITE PASTERN WHITE HEEL WHITE CORONET ERMINE MARKS

Q7.6 Describe each of these markings.

MEALY MUZZLE	
TOAD EYE	
DORSAL LINE	
ZEBRA MARKINGS	
WHORL	
INJURY MARKING	

Q7.7 List the differences and the similarities between holding a horse for treatment and standing for inspection?

DIFFERENCES

SIMILARITIES

7 ANATOMY AND HANDLING

Q7.8 List all the correct ways that this unknown horse is being led in walk.

Q7.9 List the dangers and poor practices being shown by this person trying to coax this unknown horse into trot.

Q7.10 Describe the correct way to turn a horse when led in hand.

8 HEALTH AND SAFETY

> Q8.1 List five stable-yard situations where regular lifting could be hazardous.

1. _____

2. _____

3. _____

4. _____

5. _____

> Q8.2 In the two pictures below, one shows the correct lifting method, and the other does not. Identify which is which and explain why.

8 HEALTH AND SAFETY

Q8.3 Using the words provided, complete these sentences about fitness when working on a yard.

fit   co-ordinated   safely   stresses   strains

Physical fitness is necessary to work _____ on the yard. A _____ person is likely to be stronger, more _____ and capable of carrying out yard work than someone who is not. This makes the work more efficiently achieved with fewer possibilities of _____ and _____.

Q8.4 Explain why this is the best way to carry a filled haynet.

8 HEALTH AND SAFETY

Q8.5 (a) How is a haynet weighed?
(b) Estimate the average weight of hay and haylage in the haynet sizes below.

(a)_____

(b)

SMALL HAYNET	
SMALL HAYNET WITH HAYLAGE	
LARGE HAYNET	
LARGE HAYNET WITH HAYLAGE	

Q8.6 Tying up a haynet. Describe what's happening in this sequence.

_____

_____

8 HEALTH AND SAFETY

Q8.7 List three potential dangers to the horse when using haynets.

1. _____

2. _____

3. _____

Q8.8 Prompted by the key words below, explain the benefits of using haynets.

| WEIGHT |

| SOAKING |

| WASTE |

| HYGIENIC |

| WORMS |

9 HORSE HEALTH

Q9.1 On the horse below, label the signs of good health.

Q9.2 List all the signs of poor health that you know. The drawings below hint at some of the answers.

9 HORSE HEALTH

Q9.3 Tell-tale signs in the stable and field provide indications as to the horse's health. Complete the table to explain what to look for in regard to the topics listed.

	STABLE	FIELD
FEED		
HAY		
DROPPINGS		
WATER		
BED		

Q9.4 Morning inspections include a quick look at the horse to check that he is in basic good health before he is watered, hayed and fed. List the things you would look for in this first quick check of the morning.

_____

_____

_____

_____

_____

_____

_____

_____

9 HORSE HEALTH

Q9.5 If, during your morning check, you felt that the horse was unwell, what would you do?

_____

_____

_____

_____

Q9.6 How do you check that a horse is warm enough?

_____

_____

Q9.7 Describe the signs that a horse is overweight, underweight or in good condition.

OVERWEIGHT

NECK _____

_____

_____

RIBS _____

_____

_____

QUARTERS_____

_____

_____

9 HORSE HEALTH

GOOD CONDITION

NECK _____

_____

_____

RIBS _____

_____

_____

QUARTERS _____

_____

_____

UNDER-WEIGHT

NECK _____

_____

_____

RIBS _____

_____

_____

QUARTERS _____

_____

_____

9 HORSE HEALTH

Q9.8 Listed below are statements about why you should report ill-health to a senior member of staff. Decide whether you think that they are TRUE or FALSE.

- Senior staff have more experience and can therefore make a more knowledgeable assessment.

- Senior staff have probably known the horse for longer and may have more information on the horse's medical history.

- A decision can be made quickly to give medical attention or to call the vet.

- The groom has a responsibility for the welfare of the horse in their care.

- Horses are better at healing themselves without our interference.

Q9.9 List five stable management rules which help to maintain horses in good health.

1. _____

2. _____

3. _____

4. _____

5. _____

10 HORSE BEHAVIOUR

Q10.1 Put these instincts in order of natural priority for the horse and then match them up with explanations of each by writing 1, 2 or 3 beside the explanations.

NOURISH   PROCREATE   SURVIVE

[ ] 1 → [ ] 2 → [ ] 3

Seek fresh clean water [ ]

Eat well on good grazing [ ]

Fight to stay alive if cornered [ ]

Graze [ ]

Mares come into season in spring/summer [ ]

Foals are naturally born at the time of spring grass growth [ ]

Only one stallion per herd [ ]

Run away from danger [ ]

Pass on dominant genes [ ]

Choose a variety of grasses [ ]

Remain with the herd [ ]

Nomadic [ ]

48

Q10.2 Each picture illustrates one of the horse's natural characteristics. Can you label the drawings appropriately?

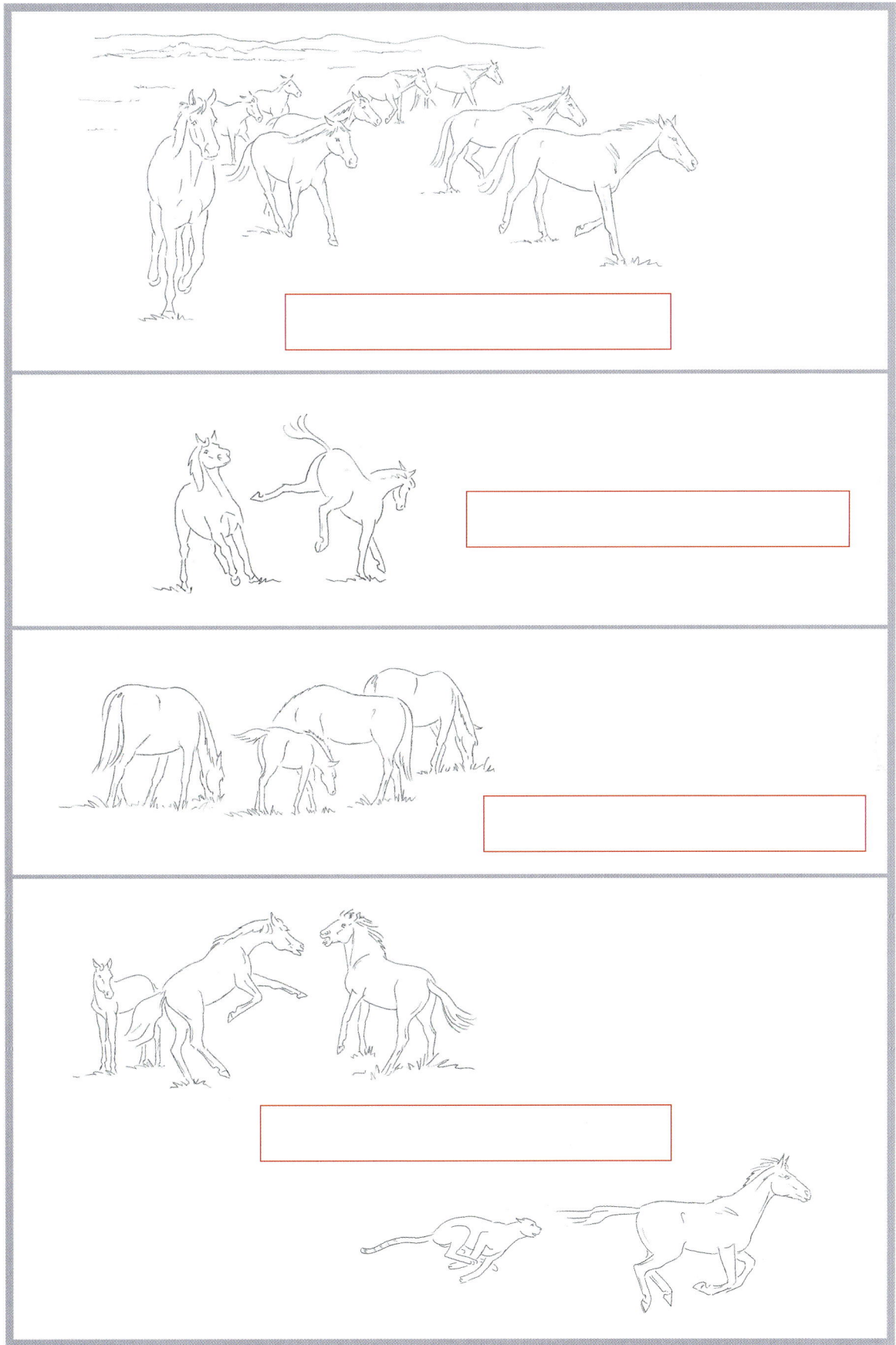

10 HORSE BEHAVIOUR

Q10.3 Match the sound to the description by drawing a line from one to the other.

WHINNY	Anger, fear, pain if mare/gelding. If from a stallion, possibly also excitement or a challenge
SCREAM	Long-distance call to gain attention, e.g. a horse on his own in a field calling to companions
SNORT	High-pitched — excitement/tension, e.g. heard from mare and foal during weaning
NEIGH	High-pitched, short sound, e.g. mare in season
SIGH	Frequent, quick nasal blows to draw in as much scent as possible, e.g. sniffing droppings of an unfamiliar horse
SNORING/ GROANING	Short, sharp sound of fear, e.g. a young horse taken on his own into an indoor school for the first time
SQUEAL	Soft, breathy sound of recognition, e.g. of a person or a horse
BLOW	Contentment, e.g. during chewing
WHICKER	Heard during sleep

10 HORSE BEHAVIOUR

Q10.4 The horse expresses himself through body language. Describe the body language /physical signs for each state, and include any special handling required, apart from normal awareness.

INTERPRETATION	BODY LANGUAGE
HAPPY	
INQUISITIVE	
PLAYFUL	
ANXIOUS	
GRUMPY	
VERY GRUMPY	

10 HORSE BEHAVIOUR

Q10.5 As a groom, you need certain qualities and know-how when handling and riding horses. Read the list below and then fit each letter appropriately into the table. If there are any traits/actions that you feel are inappropriate, underline them in red.

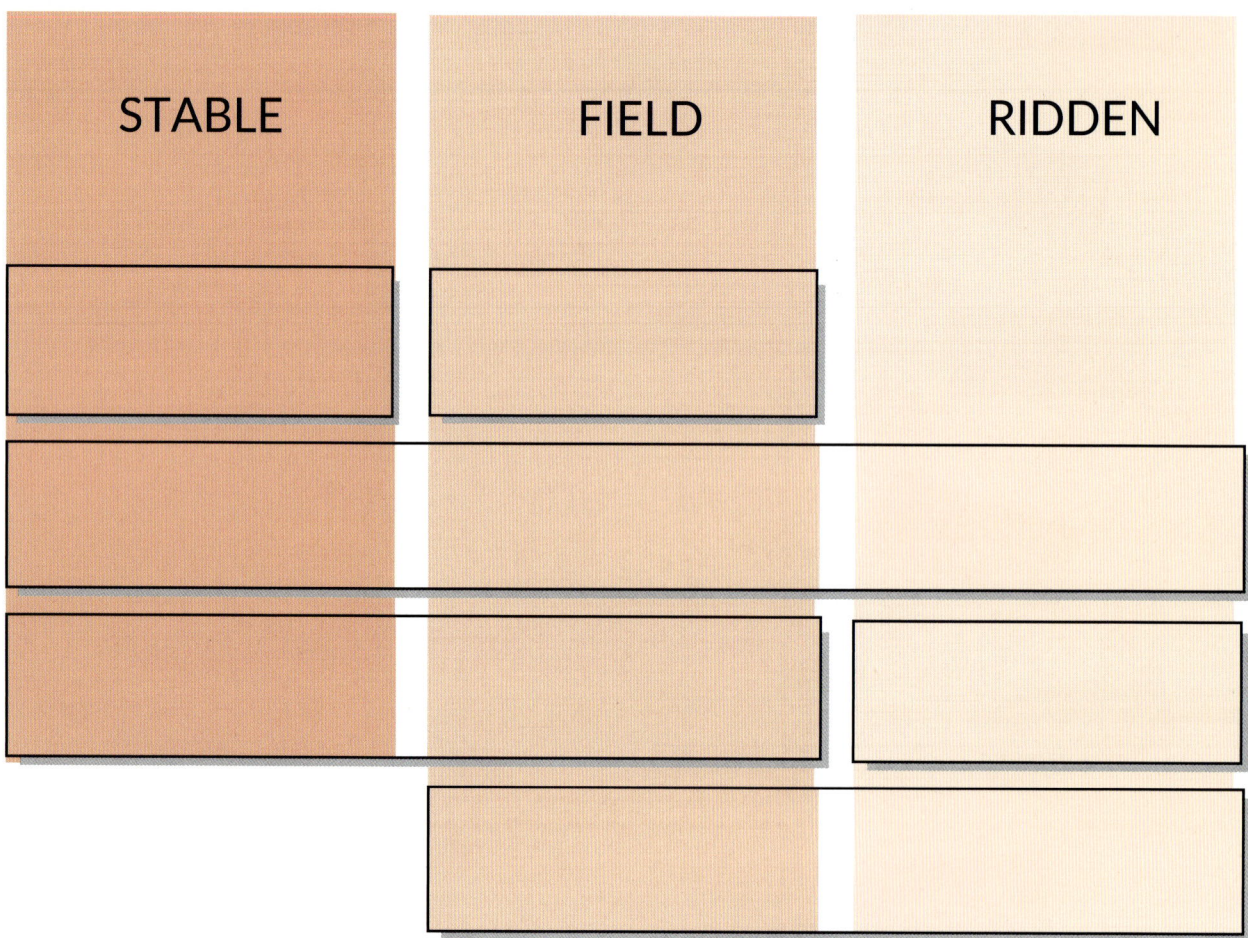

(a) Be patient.
(b) Show understanding.
(c) Never enter the stable if the horse's hind legs are facing the door.
(d) Always ensure that the horse is facing the door before you enter the stable.
(e) Whenever possible, lead from the left side.
(f) Be quick-tempered.
(g) Never carry a bucket of food into a field with more than one horse in it.
(h) Approach the horse at his shoulder.
(i) Be decisive.
(j) Ride with quiet confidence.
(k) Tie the horse up when working around him.
(l) Risk assess each situation.
(m) Ride with clarity and sympathy.
(n) Always move the horse around so that you are working in a safe space.
(o) Give clear aids/instructions.

10 HORSE BEHAVIOUR

Q10.6 Some horses can be difficult to catch in the field. List at least two methods that could be used and state how they relate to the horse's natural instincts and characteristics.

_____

_____

_____

_____

Q10.7 If you are unsure how to handle a horse that shows negative feelings, what should you do?

_____

_____

_____

Q10.8 Describe the possible signs of danger in the horse's expression and action when ridden.

	EXPRESSION
EARS	
EYES	
NOSTRILS	
LEGS	
WHOLE BODY	
TAIL	

53

11 BASIC GRASSLAND CARE

> **Q11.1** The table below lists the items that should be inspected in a field check. In each box write what you would look for and why.

FENCING	
WATER	
GATE	
SHELTER	
GRAZING	
GROUND	
POISONOUS PLANTS	

11 BASIC GRASSLAND CARE

Q11.2 Name each type of fencing and state whether it is suitable for fields with horses.

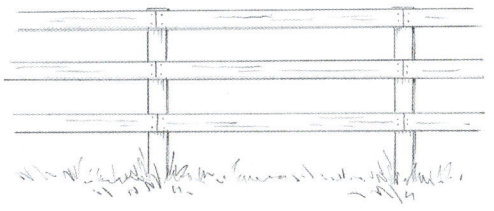

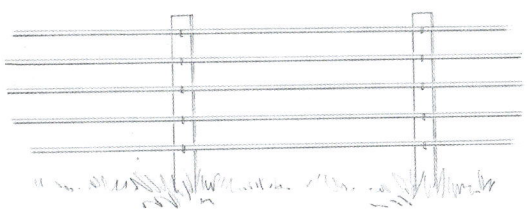

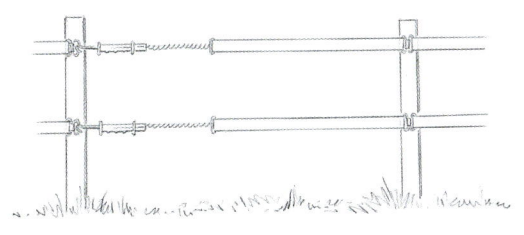

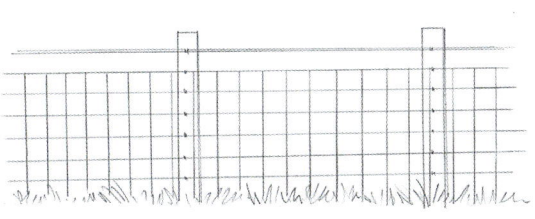

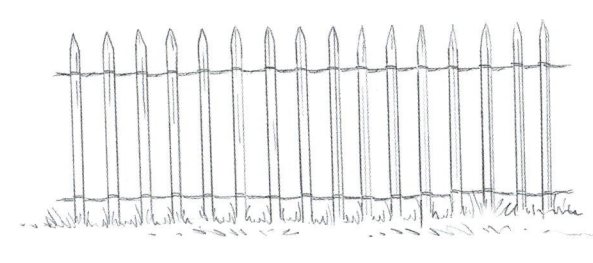

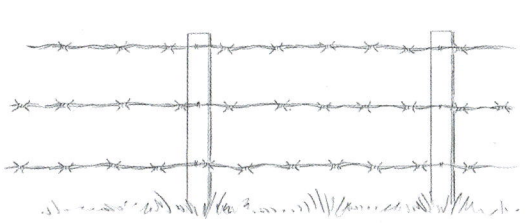

11 BASIC GRASSLAND CARE

> **Q11.3** The picture below shows a field which has not been properly maintained. Label the key factors that point to this condition.

11 BASIC GRASSLAND CARE

Q11.4 How can the undesirable field issues outlined in Q11.3 be avoided/remedied?

_____
_____
_____
_____
_____
_____
_____
_____

Q11.5 Why are droppings removed from fields?

_____
_____

Q11.6 What is the minimum recommended size of field to sustain (a) a horse (b) a pony?

(a) _____
(b) _____

Q11.7 If you had five ponies in a field, how many piles of hay would you put out and why?

_____
_____

11 BASIC GRASSLAND CARE

Q11.8 The following pictures show the correct procedure for turning a horse out into a field. Describe each picture.

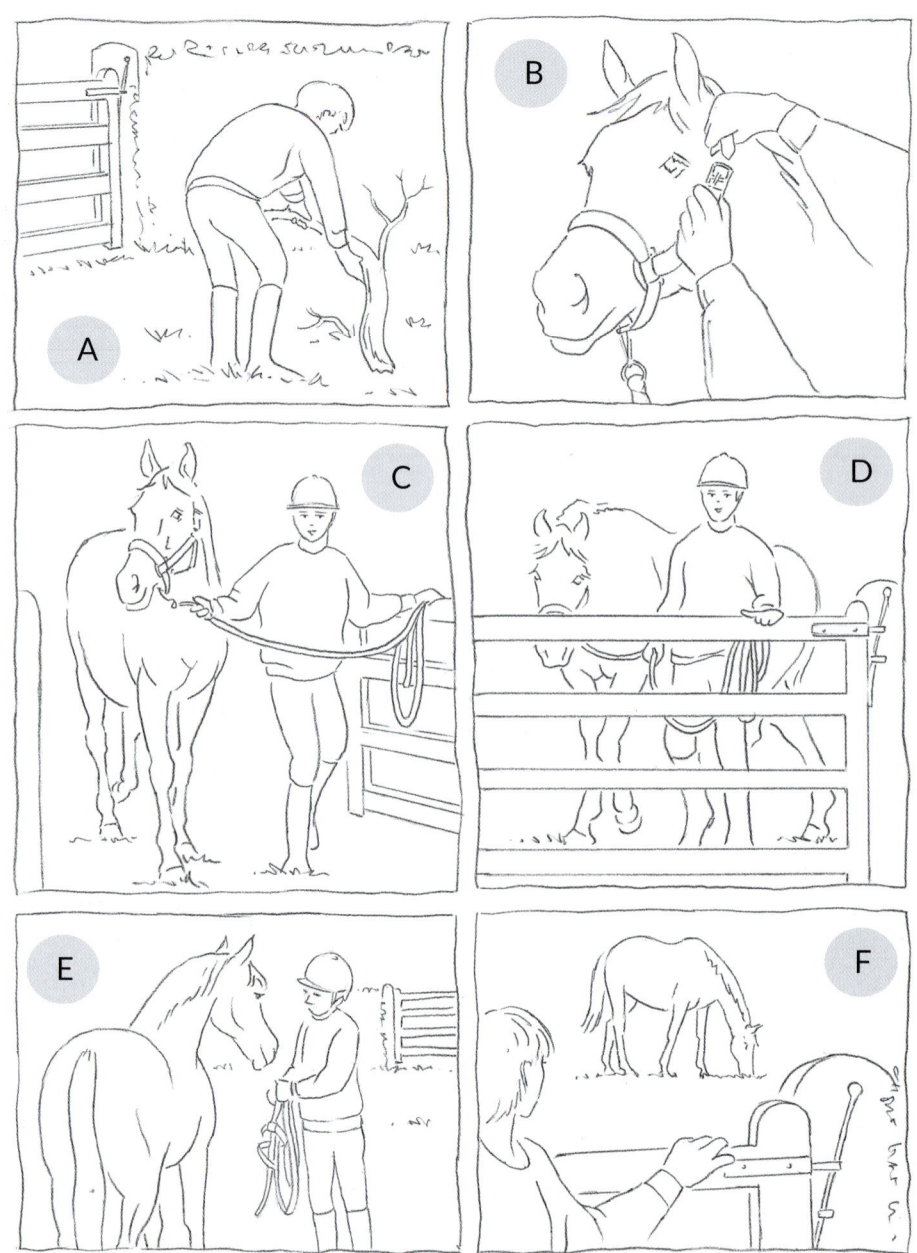

A _____

B _____

C _____

D _____

E _____

F _____

11 BASIC GRASSLAND CARE

Q11.9 The following pictures show what NOT to do when bringing a horse in from the field. List all the dangers/problems/hazards or poor practice that you can see.

A _____

B _____

C _____

D _____

E _____

F _____

G _____

12 WATERING AND FEEDING

Q12.1 Assessing hay. Complete the table with descriptions of how you would identify the quality of the hay.

	GOOD QUALITY HAY	BAD QUALITY HAY
SMELL		
COLOUR		
GRASSES		
DUST		
FEEL		

Q12.2 Hay varies in quality at different times of the year and depending on whether there was a good harvest the previous year. We know our ideal of what we would like. Now state what is acceptable, and absolutely not acceptable.

ACCEPTABLE	NOT ACCEPTABLE

Q12.3 Circle the statements that indicate good quality haylage.

- Plastic wrapping is pierced
- Good grasses
- Sweet smelling
- Dusty
- Higher moisture content than hay
- Barbed wire found in the bale
- Soggy mulch
- White areas of mould
- Separates when handled
- Golden stems
- A few docks

Q12.4 List five dangers arising from feeding poor quality hay/haylage.

_____
_____
_____
_____
_____
_____

12 WATERING AND FEEDING

Q12.5 Complete the table to list the rules of feeding and their reasons.

	RULE	REASON
FEED HORSES AS INDIVIDUALS		
QUALITY		
HYGIENE		
ROUTINE		
CHANGES		
FIBRE		
LITTLE AND OFTEN		
EXERCISE		
WATER		

12 WATERING AND FEEDING

Q12.6 The pictures show different methods of watering horses at grass. In the boxes, write the advantages and disadvantages of each.

	ADVANTAGES	DISADVANTAGES

Q12.7 Describe one method of feeding horses in the field.

_____
_____
_____
_____

63

12 WATERING AND FEEDING

Q12.8 Choosing from the feeds and forages below, circle the ones that you feel are suitable for a stabled horse or pony in light work.

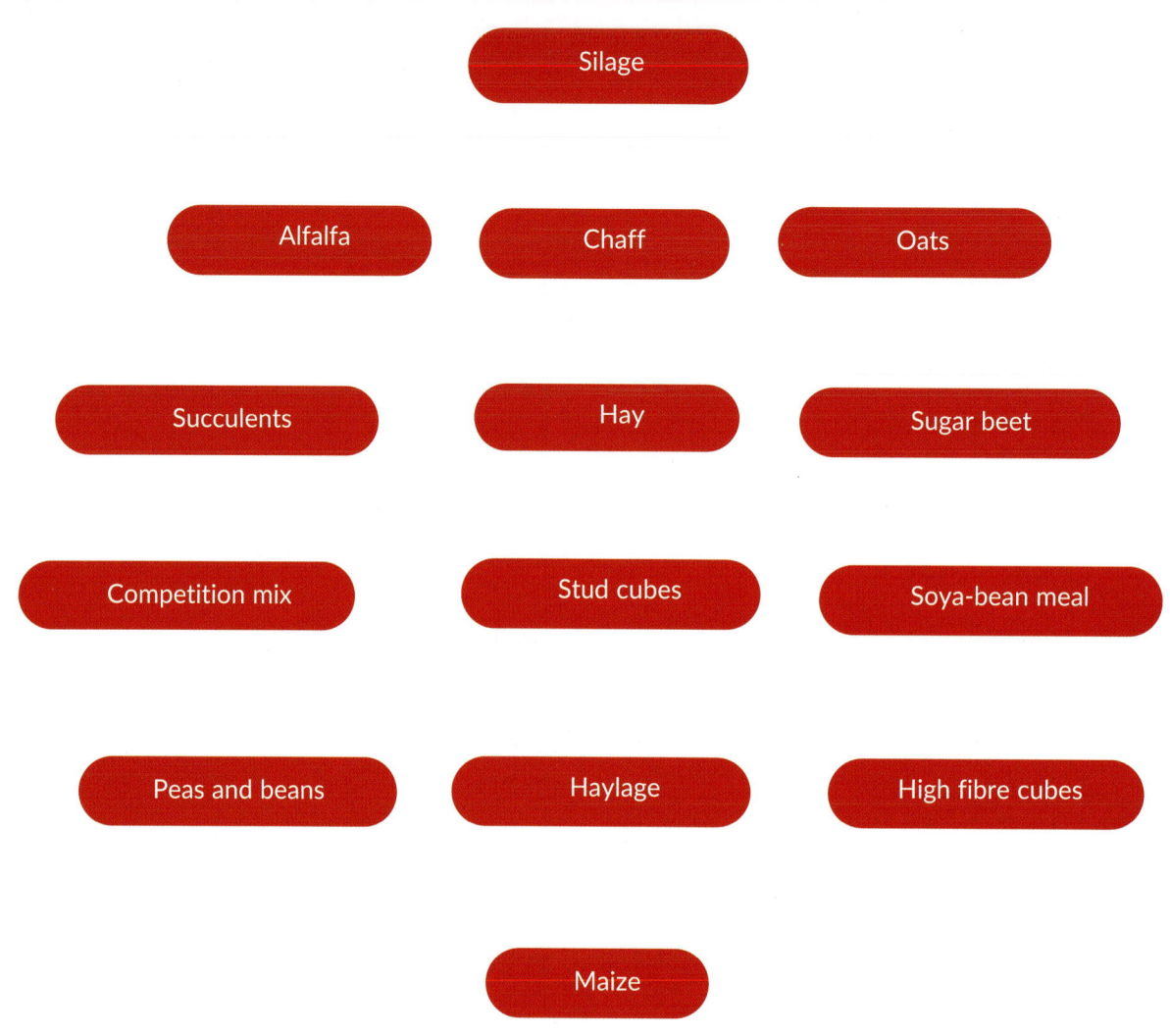

Q12.9 Sugar beet must always be soaked before being fed to horses. How long should each of the following be soaked for?

PELLETS	SHREDS	SPEEDIBEET

12 WATERING AND FEEDING

Q12.10 Write captions to the following pictures to explain how to soak a haynet.

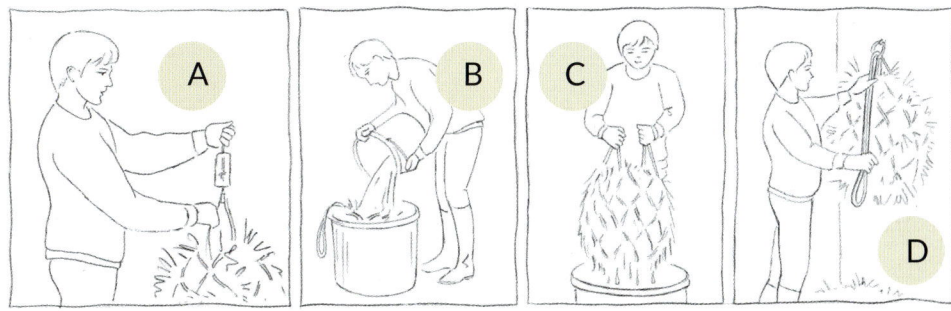

A _____

B _____

C _____

D _____

Q12.11 Circle the reasons for soaking hay.

Swells the hay seeds so they are digested, not inhaled

Washes spores away so that they are not inhaled

Makes poor, dusty hay palatable

Turns it into haylage

Prevents horses coughing

Removes nutrients from the hay for overweight horses

65

13 GENERAL KNOWLEDGE

Q13.1 Describe your responsibilities when working on a stable yard with regards to the following points.

SAFEGUARDING	
HEALTH AND SAFETY	
EQUALITY AND DIVERSITY	
DATA PROTECTION	
ANIMAL WELFARE CONCERNS	

Q13.2 Circle the clothing that you feel is appropriate for working in all weathers on the yard.

- Long-sleeved top
- Baggy trousers
- Waterproof coat
- Jewellery
- Trainers
- Jodhpurs
- Flip-flops
- Comfortable, well-fitting trousers
- Sturdy boots

13 GENERAL KNOWLEDGE

Q13.3 Circle all the fire precautions that you can see in this picture of a yard.

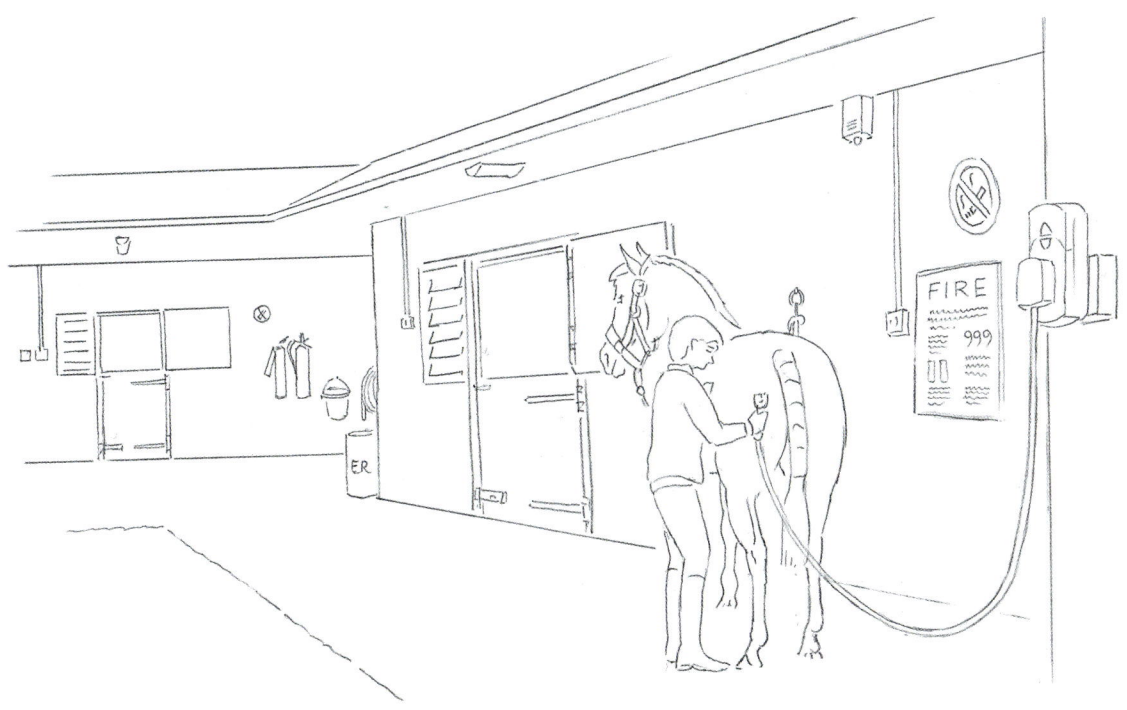

Q13.4 Describe what to do if there is an accident involving a person?

_____
_____
_____
_____
_____
_____
_____
_____

14 RIDING

Q14.1 List five safety rules for riding in a group.

_____

_____

_____

_____

_____

14.2 Riding on the road. Here we see one rider hacking and one leading. List ten rules and good practices employed when taking horses on a public highway, as depicted in the drawings.

1 _____

2 _____

3 _____

4 _____

5	
6	
7	
8	
9	
10	

Q14.3 Here is a well-dressed horse and rider, ready to ride on the highway. Label the drawing to highlight the safety aspects.

Q14.4 List the sequence for making a clear manoeuvre on the road.

14 RIDING

Q14.5 Describe the safe procedure when turning right from a minor to major road.

_____

_____

_____

_____

_____

_____

Q14.6 In the same way, describe the safe procedure when turning left from a major to minor road.

_____

_____

_____

_____

Q14.7 High visibility clothing — list three items that are available for the rider and five items for the horse.

RIDER _____

HORSE _____

_____

_____

Q14.8 Give two examples of good practice when riding on bridleways.

1. _____

2. _____

14 RIDING

> **Q14.9** From the following six pictures below and overleaf, tick the two that show how to correctly lead a tacked-up horse. Explain what is right and wrong with each of the drawings.

1 _____
_____
_____
_____

2 _____
_____

3 _____
_____
_____
_____

4 _____
_____
_____

71

14 RIDING

5 _____

6 _____

Q14.10 Before mounting, certain checks should be carried out on the horse and the tack. Label and describe the checks that you would make.

Q14.11 How can you estimate the correct length for your stirrups before mounting?

14 RIDING

Q14.12 Correct mounting sequence. Describe what's happening in each picture.

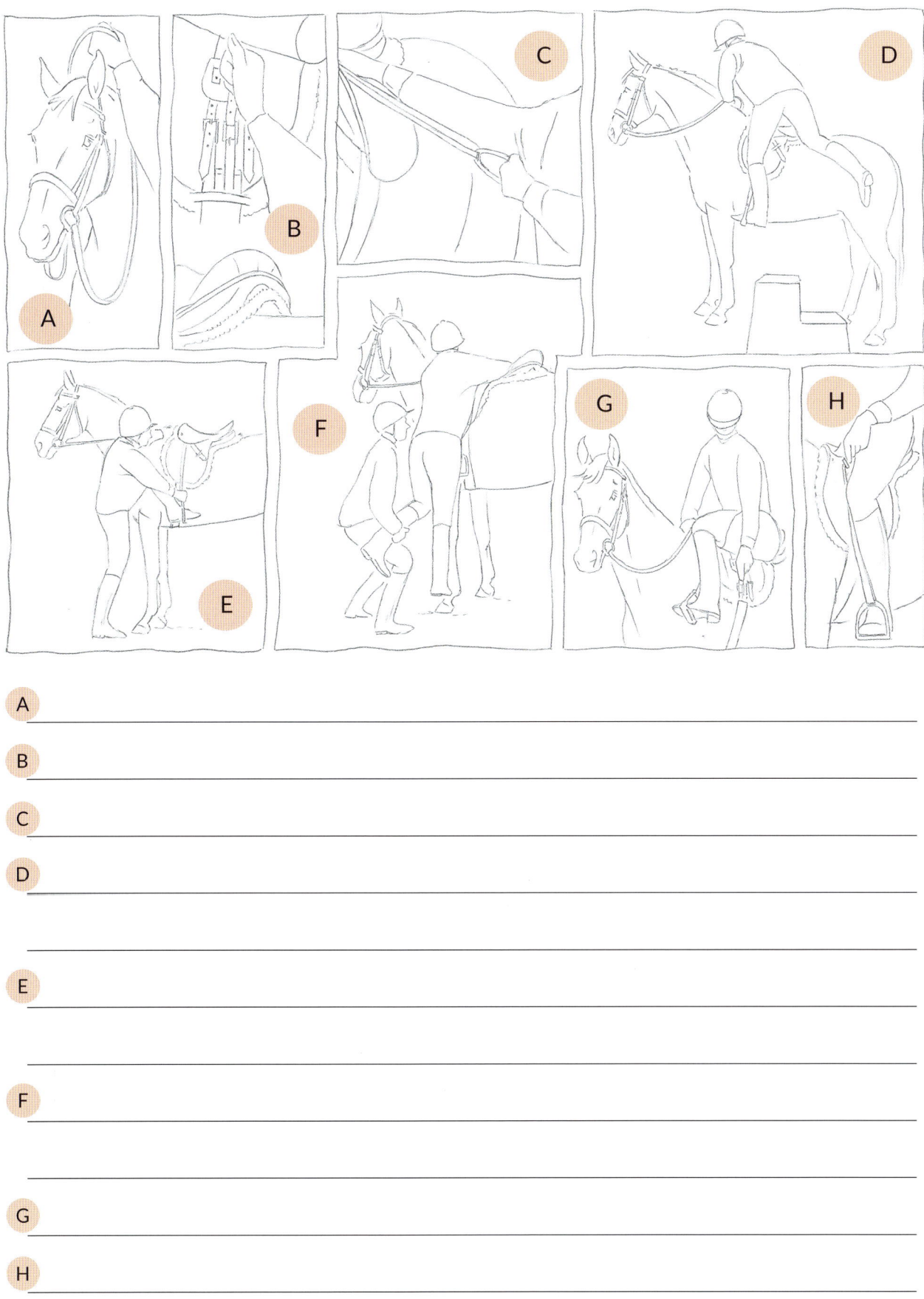

A _____

B _____

C _____

D _____

E _____

F _____

G _____

H _____

73

14 RIDING

Q14.13 From the pictures below, identify the correct positioning of stirrup and leather when ridden, and label the mistakes in the other pictures.

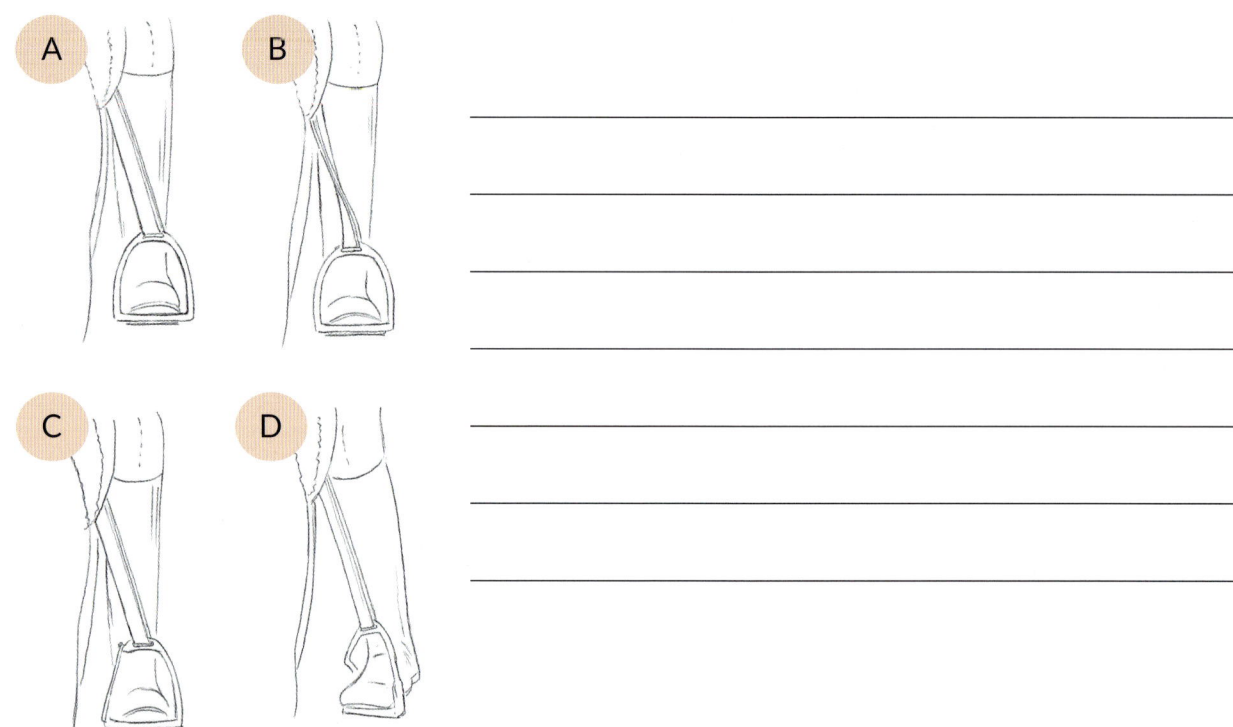

Q14.14 Mark the faults that you can spot with the horse's tack.

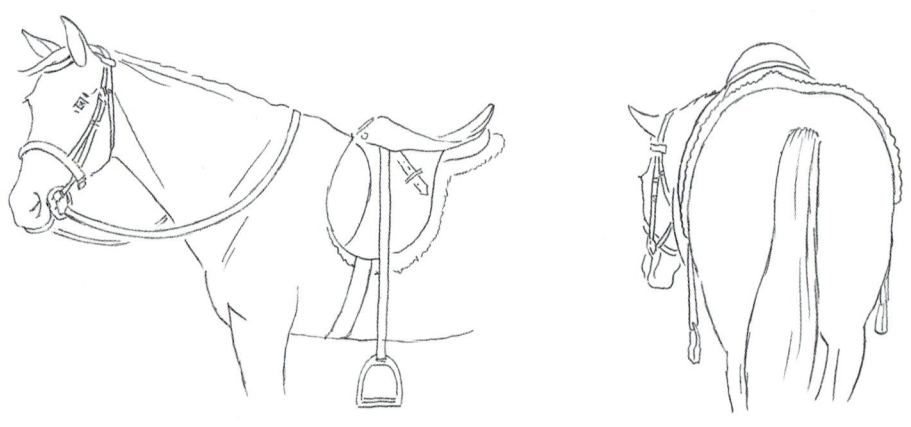

Q14.15 Add a sentence to each label to describe how to hold the reins correctly.

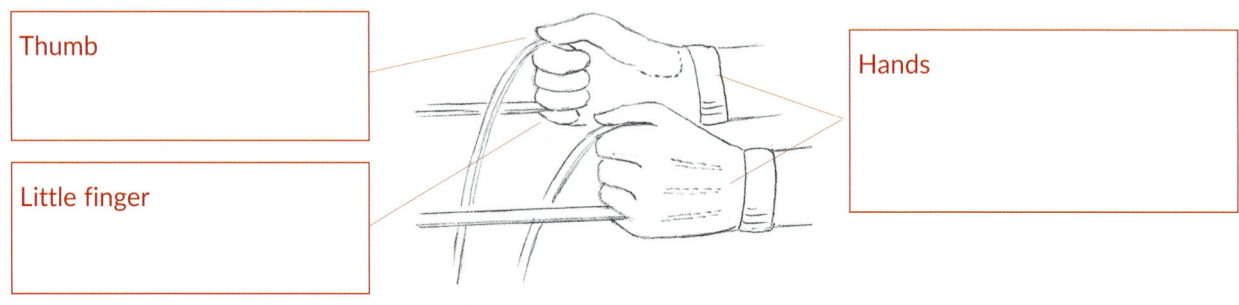

Q14.16 Describe the differences between these two images, which show good and bad position and why.

Q14.17 Fill in the gaps to describe how to change over a short whip correctly.

inside　　one　　balanced　　reins　　outside　　knee　　whip

Having changed the rein and _____ the horse, place both _____ into the _____ hand. Using the _____ hand, pull the whip through to the inside. Replace _____ rein in each hand. Position the _____ correctly over the _____.

14 RIDING

Q14.18 Number the sequence of footfall in each gait.

WALK

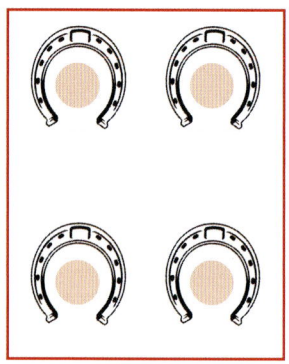

TROT

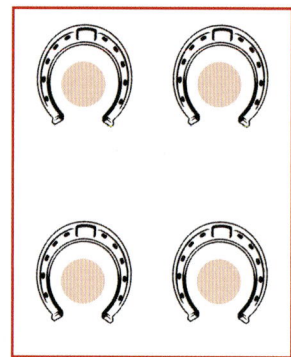

CANTER (Left)

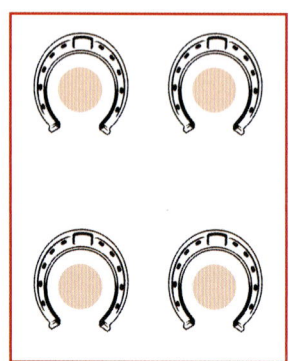

CANTER (Right)

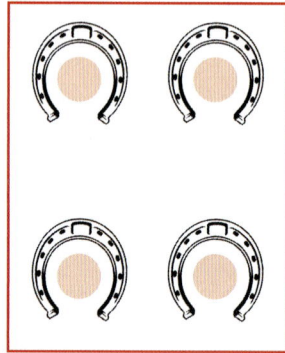

Q14.19 Write down as many of the responsibilities associated with lead file as you can think of.

_____

_____

_____

_____

_____

_____

Q14.20 Describe how to quit and cross your stirrups.

_____
_____
_____
_____
_____
_____
_____

Q14.21 Describe how each part of the body listed below should be positioned when a rider is in a light seat position.

HEAD

SHOULDERS

BACK

HIPS

KNEES

LOWER LEG

ANKLES

HEELS

14 RIDING

Q14.22 List the natural and artificial aids, and how you would apply them.

_____
_____
_____
_____
_____
_____
_____
_____
_____
_____
_____
_____

Q14.23 Fill in the gaps to complete the description of how you would recognise the correct trot diagonal, and how it helps the horse for the rider to be on the correct one.

| sitting | rising | left | balance | shoulder | feel | aids |

When riding on the left rein, the rider should be on the _____ trot diagonal. This can be recognised by looking at the horse's outside (right) _____, and with more experience, the rider will be able to _____ whether they are right or wrong. When looking at the outside shoulder, the rider should be _____ as the shoulder moves back, and _____ as it travels forwards. Being on the correct diagonal helps the horse's _____, and the co-ordination of the rider's _____.

Q14.24 Draw a different change of rein on each of these arena plans.

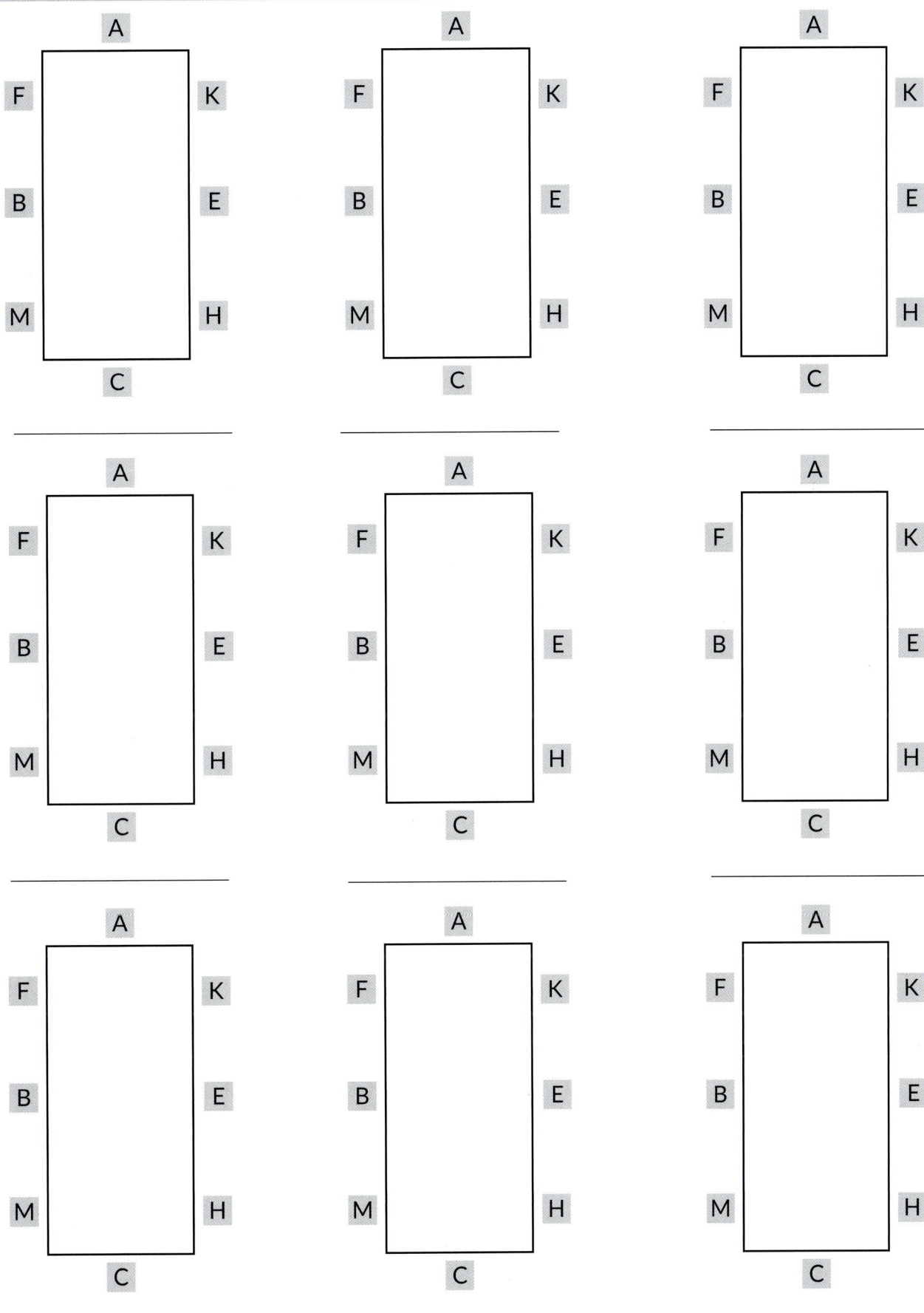

ANSWERS

ANSWERS

1 GROOMING

 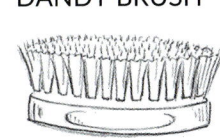 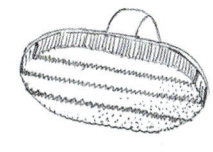

HOOF PICK   BODY BRUSH   DANDY BRUSH   PLASTIC CURRY COMB   RUBBER CURRY COMB

Q1.1

A   HOOF PICK — for cleaning out the underside of the horse's hoof.
B   BODY BRUSH — removes dried sweat and dust from the clipped, stabled horse.
C   DANDY BRUSH — removes dried sweat and mud from the field-kept, unclipped horse.
D   PLASTIC CURRY COMB — removes dried sweat and mud from the unclipped, field-kept horse. It can also be used to clean the body brush
E   RUBBER CURRY COMB — excellent at removing winter coat during the spring, mud, sweat and scurf. Used in circular motions.
F   METAL CURRY COMB — only ever used to clean brushes.
G   SWEAT SCRAPER — removes excess water on the horse's body when the horse has been washed down. Only used on large muscle areas.
H   MANE/TAIL COMB — used to comb mane and tail.
I   SPONGES — one for eyes and nose, one for dock and sheath/udders.
J   STABLE RUBBER — gives a finishing polish by removing residual dust.
K   HOOF OIL — light oil to give shine and condition to hooves.

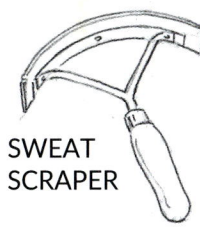

METAL CURRY COMB

Q1.2

Health — remove dust, sweat, dead skin, loose hair.
Condition — muscle tone.
Prevention of disease — helps to prevent skin diseases and parasites.
Appearance — neat, tidy and attractive.
Checking for new heat/swelling — quick and efficient treatment of new injuries.
Cleanliness — hygiene prevents sores.

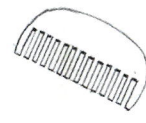

SWEAT SCRAPER

Q1.3

Quartering:
1. Tie up the horse.
2. Pick out the feet.
3. Undo and secure the rug fastenings.
4. Fold the front of the rug back.
5. Brush the front of the body and mane.
6. Fold the rear of the rug forward.
7. Brush the back of the horse.
8. Secure the rug.
9. Clean the tail.
10. Sponge eyes, nose and dock.

MANE/TAIL COMB

SPONGES

STABLE RUBBER

Q1.4

The equestrian industry wants to employ efficient staff — horses are labour intensive so staff need to work within time scales.

HOOF OIL

81

Q1.5

Horse not tied up.
Door not shut.
Picking up hind foot incorrectly.
Using metal curry comb on horse's body.
Sitting on the floor to apply hoof oil.
Front straps undone, rest of the rug still fastened.
Standing directly behind the horse to clean the dock.
Number of people (four) in the stable!

2 RUGS

Q2.1

Lightweight turnout rug with no neck cover	Use as rain sheet, help keep horse clean.
Middleweight turnout rug with detachable neck cover	Winter. Stabled horse turned out for a few hours per day. Not fully clipped.
Full neck heavyweight turnout rug	Winter. Stabled, fully clipped and turned out a few hours in the day.
Summer sheet	Keep stabled horse clean. Travelling.
Cooler rug	Cooler rug — after work/bath in warm weather.
Fleece	Fleece — wicks water away from horses's skin, help to dry off after bath or wash off after riding.
Lightweight stable rug	Stabled spring/autumn.
Heavyweight stable rug	Stabled winter.
Fly rug	Protects horse from flies and other biting insects. Can also protect against UV rays from sun.

Q2.2

1. Securely tie up the horse.
2. Place the rug over the horse's withers.
3. Fasten the front straps.
4. Unfold the rug.
5. Secure the middle straps, crossing them underneath the horse's stomach.
6. Fasten the leg straps/pull the tail over the fillet string.

Q2.3

GOOD FIT:
- Comfortable over the withers.
- Length covering the back to the top of the tail.
- Sufficient space over shoulders.
- Cross over straps adjusted correctly (should be able to fit a hand's width between belly and straps).
- Sufficient depth, covering belly.

Q2.4

POOR FIT:
- Too tight at withers.
- Too short across top of back.
- Cross over straps too tight.
- Broken straps.
- Too tight on shoulders.

Q2.5

1. Rug with leg straps fastened to the same side, having just been put on.
2. One leg strap fastened correctly around one leg.
3. Both leg straps fastened, having looped the second through the first.
4. (Incorrect) The leg straps are done up, without having looped one through the other.
5. (Incorrect) The leg straps are fastened on opposite sides.

Q2.6

All answers are TRUE

Q2.7

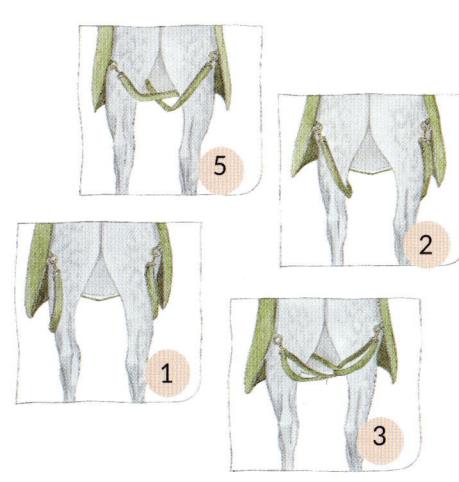
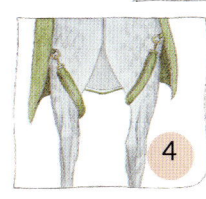
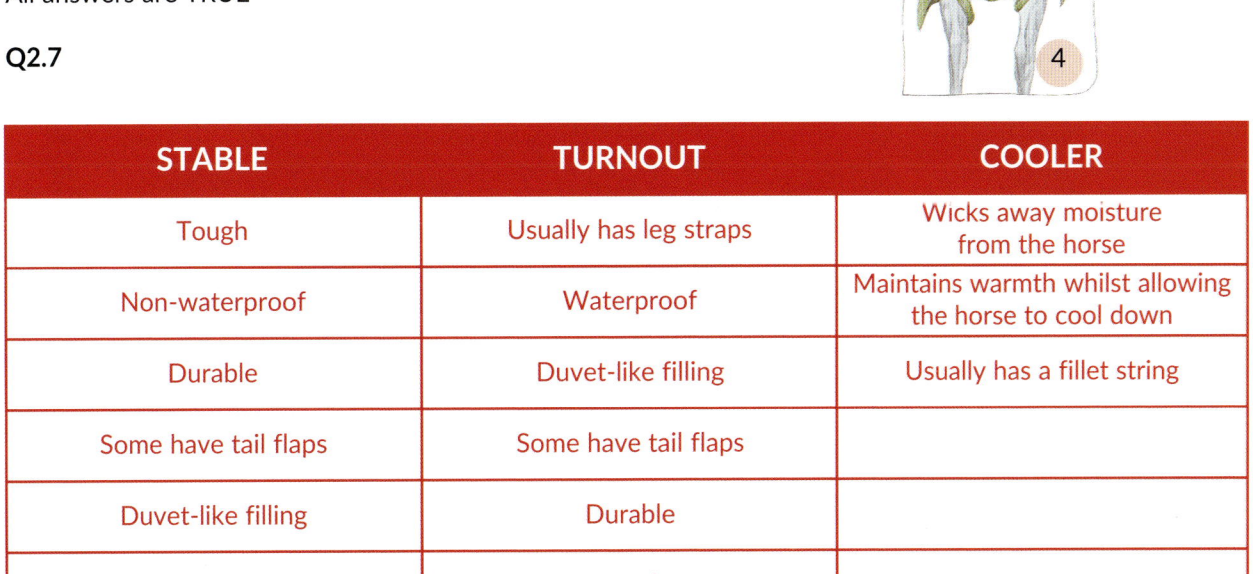

STABLE	TURNOUT	COOLER
Tough	Usually has leg straps	Wicks away moisture from the horse
Non-waterproof	Waterproof	Maintains warmth whilst allowing the horse to cool down
Durable	Duvet-like filling	Usually has a fillet string
Some have tail flaps	Some have tail flaps	
Duvet-like filling	Durable	
	Tough	

ANSWERS/3 SADDLERY

3 SADDLERY

Q3.1
Labelled saddle.

Labels: point pocket, thigh roll, knee roll, girth straps, buckle guard, pommel, seat, waist, stud, cantle, skirt, panel lining, saddle flap, cantle, panel, girth straps, gullet.

Q3.2
Labelled snaffle bridle.

Labels: headpiece, browband, cheekpieces, throatlash, noseband, snaffle bit, reins.

Q3.3
Size is appropriate. Pommel and cantle level. Numnah even under saddle, pulled up into gullet. Even-bearing surface from behind.

Q3.4

RUNNING MARTINGALE
Neckstrap joins martingale where neck meets chest.
One hand's width between neckstrap and wither.
When measured the rings of the martingale should reach the horse's throat.

STANDING MARTINGALE
Correct length measured by running the martingale up the gullet, under the jaw and to the noseband.
One hand's width between neckstrap and wither.

Q3.5

DIRTY GIRTH	Girth galls
THIN STIRRUP LEATHERS	Leathers could snap while riding
WORN STITCHING ON STIRRUP LEATHERS	Leathers could split while riding
DIRTY NUMNAH	Saddle sores
WORN STITCHES ON GIRTH STRAPS	Girth could come undone while riding

Q3.6

1. Tack collected and positioned safely.
2. Headcollar on and the groomed horse is tied up.
3. Rope looped through string; headcollar is fastened around the horse's neck.
4. Bridle is put on by sliding the bit gently into the mouth, lifting into position and sliding the headpiece over the ears.
5. The noseband is fastened and the reins twisted through the throatlash.
6. Headcollar is replaced and the horse retied.
7. The numnah is put on.
8. The saddle is positioned, pulling the numnah into the gullet of the saddle and sliding into place.
9. Moving to the offside of the horse, the girth is taken off the top of the saddle, letting it hang down.
10. The saddle is girthed up so that it remains in position, but not tight enough to mount. The buckle guards are pulled down.

ANSWERS/3 SADDLERY

Q3.7

1. Tie the horse up.
2. Undo the girth, move to the offside and place the girth over the saddle.
3. Remove the saddle, lifting it up and over.
4. Safely position the saddle out of the way.
5. Untie the horse and thread the rope through the baling twine.
6. Tie the headcollar around the horse's neck.
7. Undo the noseband and throatlash.
8. Remove the bridle, being careful not to knock the horse's teeth.
9. Replace the headcollar and retie.
10. Put the tack away neatly.

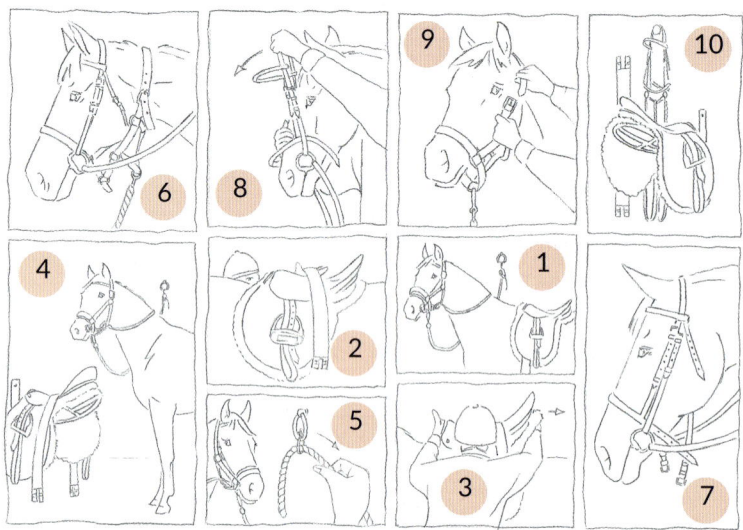

Q3.8

(a) Pony, cob, full and sometimes extra full.
(b) Place the numnah on the horse's back a little further forward than the position of the saddle. Place the saddle on top and pull the numnah up into the gullet of the saddle. Slide both saddle and numnah back into the correct position; this aids the hair to lie flat. Attach the numnah to the saddle by the loops usually positioned for the girth straps and girth.

Q3.9

Cavesson   Drop   Flash

CAVESSON — aesthetic — buckle under the jaw.
DROP — prevents the horse from opening his mouth wide enough to evade the bit — fastened under the bit with the buckle positioned so that it is not in the way of the bit or the lips.
FLASH — prevents the horse from opening his mouth wide enough to evade the bit or crossing the jaw.

Q3.10

(a) Warm water — cleans the tack — removes sweat and grime.
EITHER Oil — supples and waterproofs.
OR Saddle soap — supples, waterproofs and shines.

(b) Stripping tack, preferably weekly, enables every part of the tack to have a thorough clean and for the stitching and leather to be checked for safety. If this does not happen, areas that are not regularly oiled and soaped are likely to crack and break.

4 HANDLING

Q4.1

Stable door left open.
Tools left lying around.
Shavings bag on the floor.
Grooming kit left in middle of the walkway.
Light switch near stable.
Power point for radio near stable.
Rugs left untidily on the floor.

Q4.2

SAFETY. Of horse and groom.
RISK ASSESSMENTS. Think of potential problems as a result of an action. Try to avoid the risks. Learn to risk-assess all aspects of working with horses.
RESPECT. Respect for the horse — they are large animals. Horses must have respect for their grooms. The groom must be assertive and fair.
COMMUNICATION. For the horse to be capable of understanding what we want, we must communicate successfully. Voice and body language should reinforce each other.
DISCIPLINE. Following a routine, consistent commands and principles produce a disciplined horse.
ROUTINE. Horses thrive on routine. Try to maintain a daily routine.

Q4.3

Prepare the headcollar ready for use by unravelling the lead rope if rolled, ensuring that the noseband is done up and that the headpiece is undone. Approach the horse at his shoulder. Standing just in front of the shoulder, facing the horse's head, lift the noseband over the nose. Position the headpiece over the poll, avoiding the ears, and fasten the buckle. To check the fit, the noseband should fit two fingers' width below the projecting cheek bone and with two fingers' width between the noseband and the face.

Q4.4

(a) Baling twine, non-slip floor, no hazards for the horse in the area.
(b)

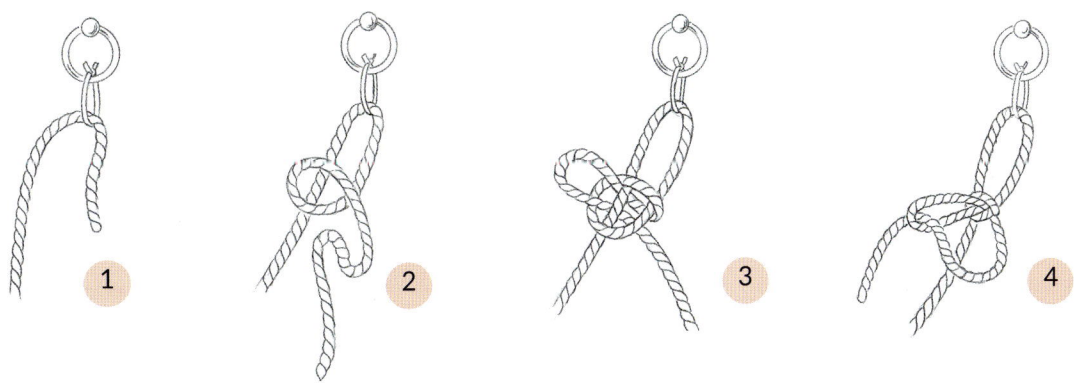

Q4.5

The equine industry requires employees who are efficient and safe. Working with horses is hard, physical work, but if a routine is worked to and everybody knows their role within a team, it can be fun and rewarding.

5 MAINTAINING CLEAN STABLES

Q5.1

BEDDING	STRAW	SHAVINGS	HEMP	PAPER	RUBBER MATTING
EXPENSIVE	Depends on season	Yes	Yes	Yes unless collected as waste product	Initial cost
EDIBLE	Yes	No	No	No	No
EASY STORAGE	Need barn	Yes	Yes	Yes	N/A
EASY DISPOSAL	Yes	Not always — long time to rot	Yes	Not always — depends	Yes — less waste
DUSTY	Possibly	Possibly but can buy dust free shavings	No	No	No
COMFORT	Yes	Yes	Can have sharp shards	Yes	No
CLEAN	Yes	Yes	Yes	No	Always use with bedding

Q5.2

Stale/urinate — horses prefer to urinate on bedding/grass rather than on a hard floor; lie down — for rest and relaxation; roll — for enjoyment or if sweaty/wet. Warmth and protection — to ensure horse stays warm in winter and to protect him from injury.

Q5.3

Although types of bedding vary, maintenance is fairly similar. They are all generally mucked out daily and skipped out every time you enter the stable. Day beds tend to be thinner, with the bedding thrown up into the banks. More bedding may be added to night beds so that the horse has a thicker bed in which to lie down at night. Banks are built to stop draughts and to prevent the horse from becoming cast.

Q5.4

ADVANTAGES	DISADVANTAGES
DAILY MUCKING OUT	
• Clean, dry bed • Horses' feet are likely to remain clean and dry	• Labour intensive
DEEP LITTERING	
• Quick to manage, on a daily basis • Offers a warm, thick, non-slip base to the bed	• Labour intensive when dug out weekly • Particular attention needs to be paid to the health of the foot as more prone to induce thrush

Q5.5

1. Remove the horse from the stable or tie up securely.
2. Remove the water buckets.
3. Remove the droppings.
4. Remove the wet area, sorting it from the clean.
5. Throw all bedding up one or two banks (rotated daily).
6. Sweep the floor.
7. Lay the bed.
8. Replace the freshly filled water buckets.

ANSWERS/6 THE FOOT AND SHOEING

Q5.6

SKIP OUT — Remove droppings, reshape banks, sweep front of the bed back, check water supply clean and full, check haynet safe and refill if required.

Q5.7

Three heaps:
- One well rotted and ready to be taken away as manure.
- One in the process of rotting.
- One in use. This must be maintained daily to prevent unnecessary spread of the area.

All should be built square and kept well trodden down to keep the air out, minimising fire risk.

Q5.8

Wheelbarrow the wrong way around.
Tossing muck from behind/underneath the horse.
Other tools left inside the stable.
Haynet on the floor.

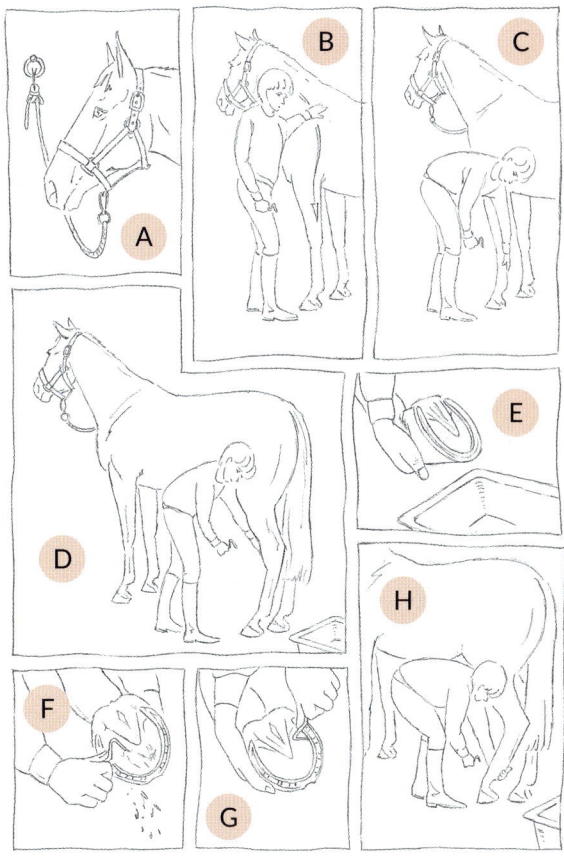

6 THE FOOT AND SHOEING

Q6.1

A Horse tied up securely.
B Start at the front and run the hand down the neck, shoulder and foreleg.
C For the front leg, run the hand down the back of the leg.
D For the back leg, run the hand down the front of the leg. Therefore the arm bends in the direction of the leg.
E The leg is held into the body and supported underneath the hoof and pastern.
F Pick out the feet using a downward movement with the hoof pick. Start at the heel and run down each lateral cleft, avoiding the soft, sensitive frog.
G Clean out the sole area, checking the shoe at the same time.
H Gently place the foot on the ground.

Q6.2

Using a water brush, clean the outside of the hooves. Pick up each foot in turn and gently scrub the underside of each hoof. Once the feet are dry, oil inside and out using hoof oil or dressing.

Q6.3

Recently shod — shod one or two weeks ago.
In need of shoeing — the foot requires attention.
Risen clenches — as the toe grows, it takes the shoe forwards causing the clenches to rise.
Twisted shoe — the shoe is not flat on the horse's foot; it may be pulled away from the foot and be bent.
Loose shoe — movement of the shoe when examined.
Cast shoe — the shoe has come off.
Worn thin — thin, wafer-like shoes that may actually snap.
Long feet — many horses grow more at the toe than at the heel and therefore give the impression of long toes.
Overgrown foot — growth over the sides of the shoe.

ANSWERS / 7 ANATOMY AND HANDLING

Q6.4

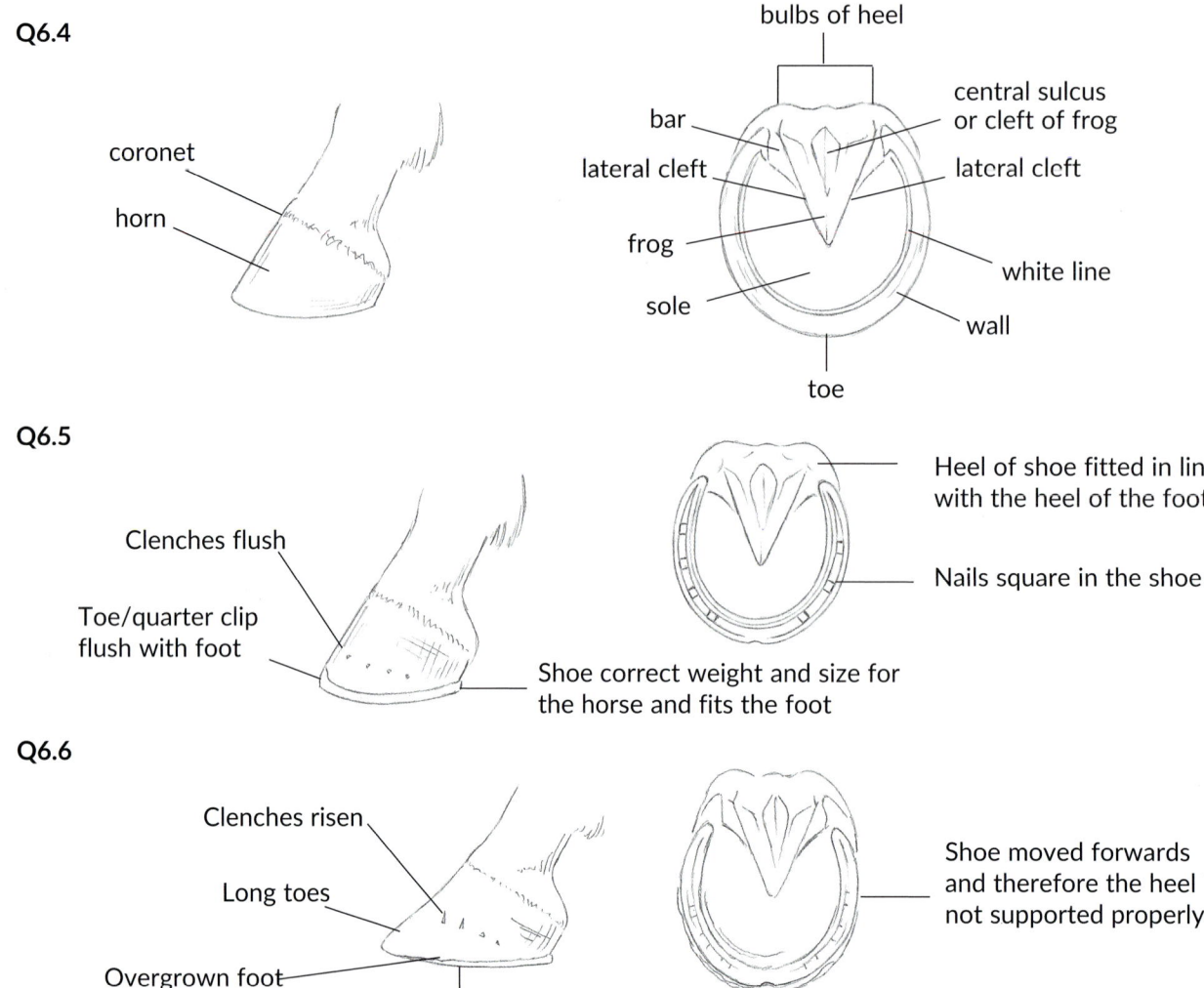

Q6.5

Q6.6

7 ANATOMY AND HANDLING

Q7.1

A Forelock	I Point of elbow	Q Stifle
B Muzzle	J Chestnut	R Back
C Jugular groove	K Pastern	S Withers
D Forearm	L Hock	T Crest
E Knee	M Point of buttock	U Poll
F Coronet	N Dock	V Shoulder
G Hoof	O Point of hip	
H Fetlock	P Croup	

Q7.2

BAY	Brown (any shade) body with black mane, tail and legs.
GREY	White/grey all over.
CHESTNUT	Chestnut all over.
BLACK	Black all over.
BROWN	Brown all over.
DUN	Sandy body with black mane, tail and legs.
PALOMINO	Sandy body with cream/white mane and tail.
PIEBALD	Black and white all over.
SKEWBALD	White with patches of any other colour apart from black.
SPOTTED	White with black spots or dark with white spots.
ROAN	Base colour of chestnut, bay, or grey with flecks of white all over.

ANSWERS / 7 ANATOMY AND HANDLING

Q7.3

GREY: Flea bitten,  Iron grey,  Dapple

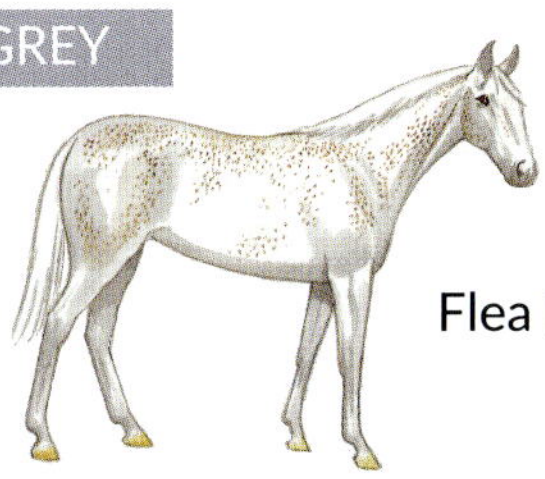

SPOTTED: Leopard spotted,  Blanket spotted

Q7.4

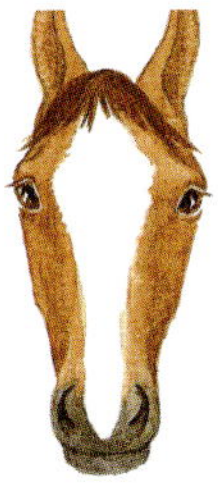

Blaze, 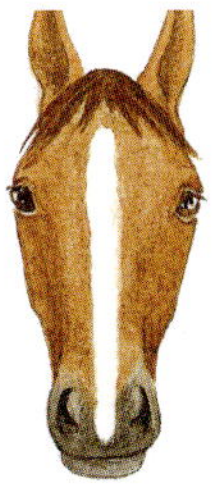 Stripe, 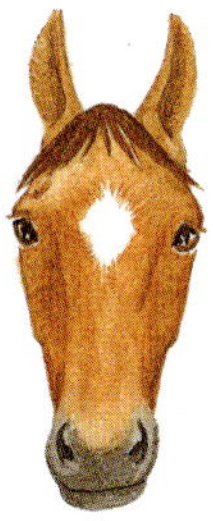 Star,  White lip,  White muzzle,  Snip

Q7.5

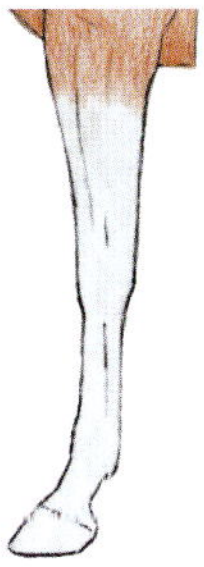

White to elbow, 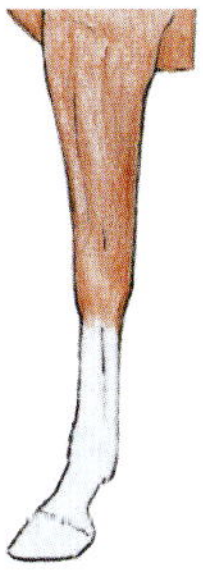 White to knee, 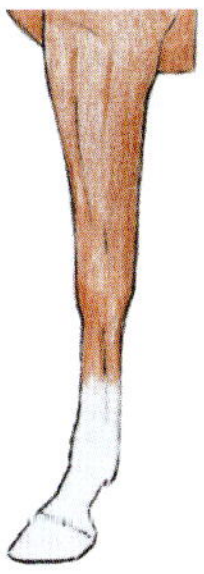 White to mid cannon, 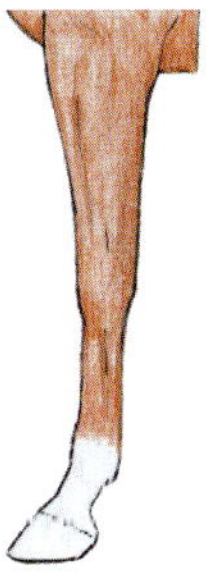 White fetlock, 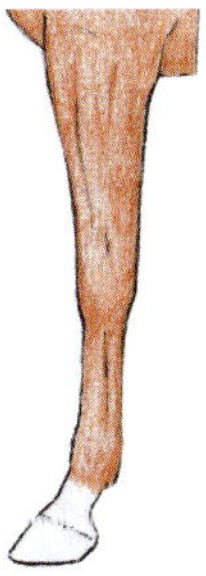 White pastern, 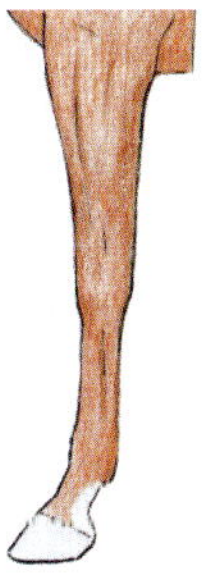 White heel, 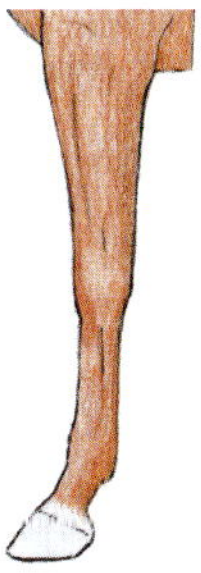 White coronet, 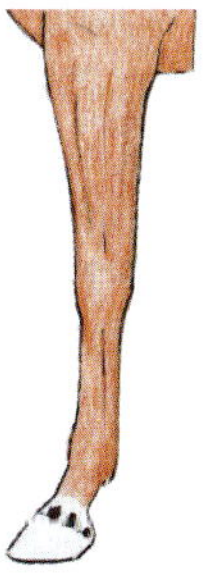 Ermine marks

Q7.6

Mealy muzzle	Lighter around the muzzle
Toad eye	Lighter around the eye
Dorsal line	Darker stripe down the spine
Zebra markings	Stripes on the legs
Whorl	Circular ring of hair with a definite centre
Injury marking	Area of trauma identified from the white hairs which grow at the site of injury

ANSWERS/8 HEALTH AND SAFETY

Q7.7

DIFFERENCES
The horse can be anxious about treatments and not about inspections.
The inspection is usually carried out on hard, level ground and the horse must be standing squarely.
Treatment may be in a loosebox.
Stand slightly forward of the horse, but to the side for an inspection, so the viewer can see the whole horse.

SIMILARITIES
Always on the same side as the person treating or inspecting the horse. This way you are aware if they are likely to do anything which will make the horse react. Try to keep the horse calm. A bridle may be necessary to help with control.

Q7.8

Hat and gloves.
Whip in left hand.
Bridle.
Holding the reins correctly.
Led at the horse's shoulder.
Freedom for the horse to move his head naturally, but enough control to keep the horse straight.

Q7.9

In front of the horse.
Facing the horse.
Shouting at the horse.
Waving the whip.
No hat/gloves.
Headcollar, not bridle.

Q7.10

In walk, turn the horse away from you, so that you are on the outside of the horse. This gives you greater control and prevents your feet from being trodden on. Walk a comfortable size turn for the horse.

8 HEALTH AND SAFETY

Q8.1

Carrying tack.
Saddling a large horse.
Lifting a filled haynet.
Moving small bales of hay/straw.
Lifting up a heavy wheelbarrow.

Q8.2

Bad:
Legs straight.
Object far away.
Lifting like this will place strain on the back.

Good:
Keep back straight.
Get close to the object to be lifted.
Bend knees and gain good purchase on the object.
During the lift, take the strain on the legs, not the back.

Q8.3

Physical fitness is necessary to work safely on the yard. A fit person is likely to be stronger, more co-ordinated and capable of carrying out yard work than someone who is not. This makes the work more efficiently achieved with fewer possibilities of stresses and strains.

Q8.4

Straight back.
The haynet is carried in the centre of the back with the weight of the net running through the legs and feet.

Q8.5

a) Spring balance.

b)

Small haynet	1–1.5kg (2–3lbs)
Small haynet with haylage	2–2.5kg (4–5lbs)
Large haynet	3–4.5kg (6–9lbs)
Large haynet with haylage	6–7.5kg (12–15lbs)

Q8.6

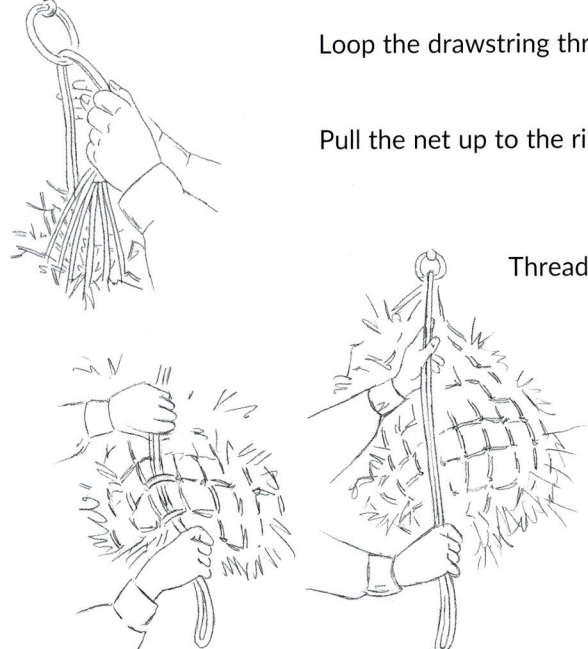

Loop the drawstring through the tie-ring.

Pull the net up to the ring.

Thread the drawstring through the bottom of the net . . .

. . . and pull the bottom up as high as possible.

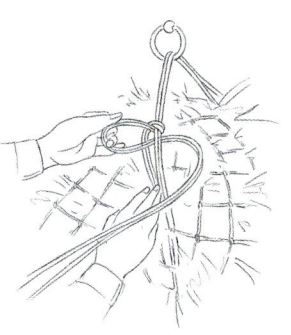

Secure with a quick-release knot.

Turn the net over so that the knot is on the underside.

Q8.7

The knot is pulled loose by the horse, releasing the net onto the floor.
The net is tied too low and the horse's legs/feet become caught in the net.
The haynet can become tangled up with the teeth.

Q8.8

WEIGHT — using a spring balance, it is possible to be very accurate with the amount of hay given.
SOAKING — easy to soak/dampen hay.
WASTE — less wasteful than feeding off the floor.
HYGIENIC — more hygienic than feeding on the floor.
WORMS — less likelihood of transferring worm burden if a stable is used alternately by different horses.

9 HORSE HEALTH

Q9.1

Behaving normally.
Bright, alert, relaxed.
Shiny coat.
Eyes and nose free from discharge.
Standing squarely — sometimes resting a hind leg, but never a foreleg.

+ if in field: grazing, with the herd, looks sound when moves.

Q9.2

Dull, lethargic.
Head down, droopy.
Dull, staring coat.
'Tucked up' — abdomen lifted and hollow flanks.
Not square in stance.
Frequent rolling.

+ if in field: not grazing, away from the herd, lying down for a long period.

Q9.3

STABLE	FIELD
Feed eaten	Feed eaten (if fed in field)
Hay eaten	Hay eaten (if only in field in winter with piles of hay)
Droppings normal number (8–12 per day) and consistency (break on landing on the ground)	If in herd, cannot identify individual droppings
Water drunk — not possible to see with automatic waterers unless metered	Can only check consumption if buckets/butt filled manually and only one horse in the field
Normal bed — messy if normally messy, clean if normally clean	N/A

Q9.4

Bright, alert, looking for food.
Normal breathing.
No discharge.
Standing squarely.
Bed and droppings normal.
Hay/feed eaten and water drunk.

Q9.5

Report immediately to a senior member of staff.

Q9.6

Feel the base of the horse's ears.

Q9.7

OVERWEIGHT	Neck	Fat hump or solid fat stored at crest
	Ribs	Cannot feel ribs, fat deposits over and between ribs
	Quarters	No definition of hips, fat stored either side of spine creating a channel running down the spine
GOOD CONDITION	Neck	Thin layer of fat under the skin, some top line
	Ribs	Ribs not visible but can be easily felt (although it can be normal to see ribs on some horses e.g. fit horses)
	Quarters	Rump rounded, hips bones just visible
UNDERWEIGHT	Neck	Narrow neck with no fat covering
	Ribs	Spine, withers, shoulders and ribs clearly visible
	Quarters	Hip bones clearly visible, outline of quarters is hollow and falling away

Q9.8

- Senior staff have more experience and can therefore make a more knowledgeable assessment. TRUE.
- Senior staff have probably known the horse for longer and may have more information on the horse's medical history. TRUE.
- A decision can be made quickly to give medical attention or to call the vet. TRUE.
- The groom has a responsibility for the welfare of the horse in their care. TRUE.
- Horses are better at healing themselves without our interference. FALSE.

Q9.9

- Check the horse regularly.
- Worm regularly.
- Shoe regularly.
- Keep to a routine.
- Vaccinate regularly.
- Feed correctly.
- Exercise correctly.
- Check that the horse has a safe environment — stable, field, arena.

10 HORSE BEHAVIOUR

Q10.1

1. Survive.
2. Nourish.
3. Procreate.

Remain with the herd. 1
Fight to stay alive if cornered. 1
Run away from danger. 1
Graze. 2
Nomadic. 2
Eat well on good grazing. 2
Choose a variety of grasses. 2
Foals are naturally born at the time of spring grass growth. 2
Seek fresh, clean water. 1
Only one stallion per herd. 3
Pass on dominant genes. 3
Mares come into season in spring/summer. 3

ANSWERS/10 HORSE BEHAVIOUR

Q10.2

| HERD ANIMAL | PECKING ORDER | GRAZER | FIGHT OR FLIGHT |

Q10.3

SCREAM	Anger, fear, pain if mare/gelding. If a stallion, possibly also excitement or a challenge.
NEIGH	Long-distance call to gain attention, e.g. a horse on his own in a field calling to companions.
WHINNY	High-pitched — excitement/tension, e.g. heard from mare and foal during weaning.
SQUEAL	High-pitched, short sound, e.g. mare in season.
BLOW	Frequent, quick nasal blows to draw in as much scent as possible, e.g. sniffing droppings of an unfamiliar horse.
SNORT	Short, sharp sound of fear, e.g. a young horse taken on his own into an indoor school for the first time.
WHICKER	Soft, breathy sound of recognition, e.g. of a person or horse.
SIGH	Contentment, e.g. during chewing.
SNORING/GROANING	Heard during sleep.

Q10.4

INTERPRETATION	BODY LANGUAGE
HAPPY	Ears forward
INQUISITIVE	Head up, ears forward, snorting; horse may spook
PLAYFUL	Ears forward; quick movements; horse may nip/kick in play
ANXIOUS	Ears moving, head up, tense; may be unpredictable
GRUMPY	Ears back; may be aggressive
VERY GRUMPY	Ears back; threatening behaviour; seek assistance in handling

Q10.5

STABLE	FIELD	RIDDEN
(c) (d) (k)	(g)	
(a)	(b) (i) (l)	(o)
(h)	(n)	(j) (m)
(f)	(e)	

ANSWERS / 11 BASIC GRASSLAND CARE

Q10.6

1. Remove other horses from the field first. HERD ANIMAL
2. Pretend to play with something in the field. CURIOSITY
3. Turn out on own and use feed bowl with food to entice. NOURISHMENT
4. Have feed ready in stable. NOURISHMENT
5. Turn out with well-fitting field safe headcollar. OVERCOME FLIGHT INSTINCT
6. Turn out in small grazing paddock. NOURISHMENT
7. Don't always work after catching. CREATURES OF HABIT — ASSOCIATING CATCHING WITH WORK

Q10.7

Ask a senior member of staff to demonstrate how to deal with the situation.

Q10.8

	EXPRESSION
EARS	Back, rotating
EYES	Wild, rolling, showing whites
NOSTRILS	Flared, snorting
LEGS	Will not halt, fidgets
WHOLE BODY	Tense, shakes
TAIL	Swishing

11 BASIC GRASSLAND CARE

Q11.1

FENCING	Secure. Report broken areas. Use electrical tester to check electric fencing. Fencing keeps horses securely in the field.
WATER	Clean, fresh, constant supply available. Check automatic trough works. Water is essential for life.
GATE	Hangs properly and opens and closes well. Normally secured both sides to prevent thieves from taking the gate off its hinges. Gate is required for safe access in and out of the field.
SHELTER	In sound condition. Provides shelter from inclement weather. Possibly a thick hedge.
GRAZING	Not too sparse/too much. Food is essential for life.
GROUND	Flat, not rutted. Do not want to put unnecessary stresses on the horse's limbs.
POISONOUS PLANTS	Ragwort, deadly nightshade, foxglove, buttercup, oak, yew, sycamore. These can be fatal if ingested.

Q11.2

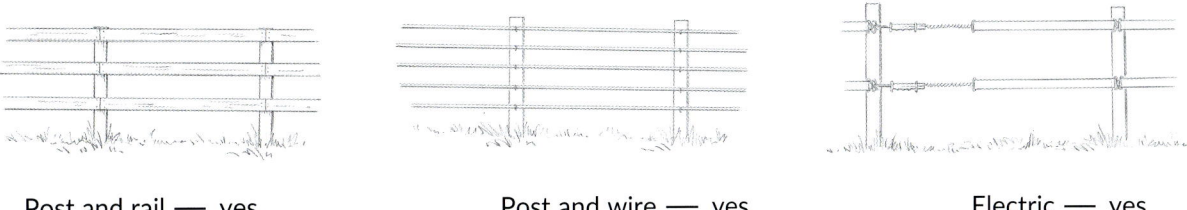

Post and rail — yes   Post and wire — yes   Electric — yes

ANSWERS/11 BASIC GRASSLAND CARE

Hedges — yes, but must be dense, high enough and free from poisonous plants

Walls — yes, but need to be high enough

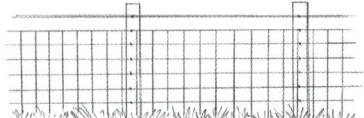

Pig netting — no

Sheep stakes — no

Barbed wire — no

Q11.3

- Excess droppings on the ground.
- Roughs (areas of sour, rank grasses because the horses produce droppings there) and lawns (areas of good, palatable grasses).
- Little/no grass and many weeds.
- Fencing in poor condition.
- Water trough of foul water and algae.
- Ground by the gate is poached.

Q11.4

Pick up droppings daily.
Implement a good seasonal grassland management plan to roll, harrow, seed, fertilise and weed-kill the fields.
Do not overstock the fields.
Clean water troughs regularly.
Maintain fencing.

Q11.5

To prevent the spread of worms and to allow palatable, good grasses to grow.

Q11.6

Horse — $1^{1}/_{2}$–2 acres. Pony — 1 acre.

Q11.7

6–7 piles, well spaced out — to prevent arguments.

Q11.8

A Check that the route is free from hazards.
B Securely fasten the headcollar on the horse.
C Lead the horse correctly and quietly to the field.
D Lead the horse into the field. Turn him around and shut the gate.
E Turn him around and remove the headcollar.
F Leave the field and securely fasten the gate.

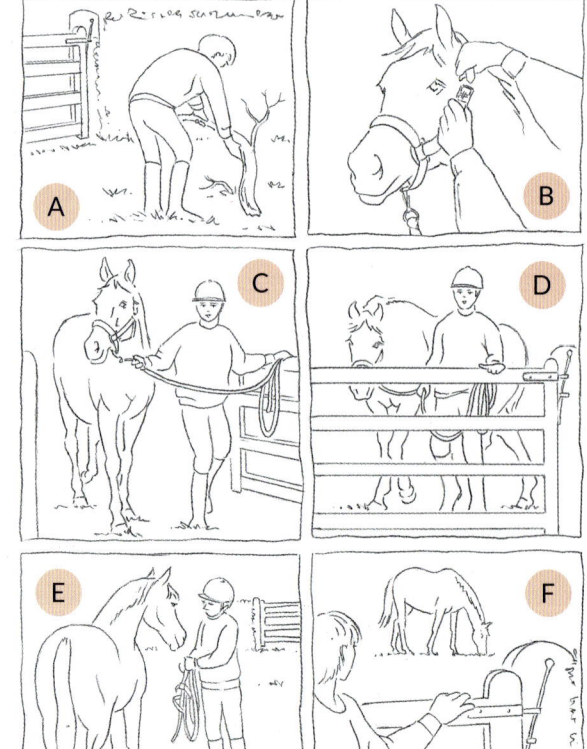

Q11.9

A Entering the field with a bucket of nuts.
B Leaving the gate open a little.
C Running towards the horse.
D Not fastening the headcollar properly.
E Leading in front of the horse, on the mobile phone.
F Pushing the gate shut as the horse walks through, almost catching the horse's hind legs.
G Dogs, children and cars — and still not leading properly even though horse looks anxious.

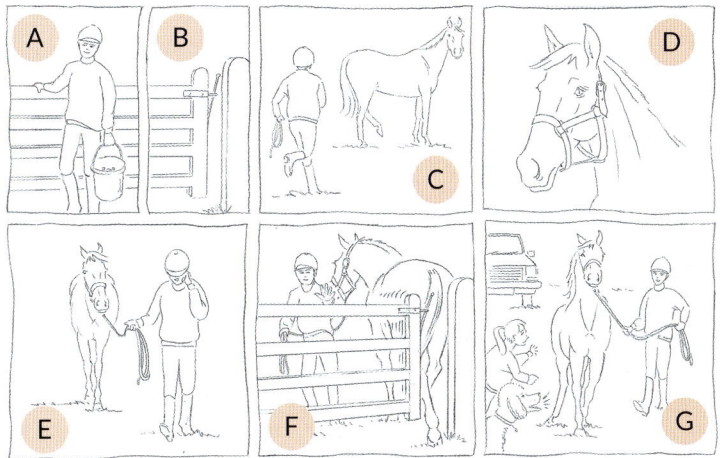

12 WATERING AND FEEDING

Q12.1

	GOOD QUALITY HAY	BAD QUALITY HAY
SMELL	Sweet	Sour and damp
COLOUR	Golden/green	Black, dark brown
GRASSES	Quality grasses, no poisonous plants	Weeds, poisonous plants, poor grasses
DUST	No dust	Dusty
FEEL	Dry, crisp	Damp, soggy

Q12.2

ACCEPTABLE	NOT ACCEPTABLE
Sweet smell	Smells musty
Golden colour	Brown/grey colour
Variety of grasses	Weeds or poisonous plants
Not dusty	Dusty
Dry	Damp and soggy

ANSWERS/12 WATERING AND FEEDING

Q12.3

Higher moisture content than hay.
Sweet smelling.
Separates when handled.
Golden stems.
Good grasses.

Q12.4

Respiratory problems.
Weight loss due to lack of nutrients or not eating.
Toxicity from poisonous plants, especially ragwort.
Scouring.
Sores in the corners of the mouth — occurs when grasses are hard and dry.
Colic.
Botulism — from poorly made haylage.

Q12.5

	RULE	REASON
FEED HORSES AS INDIVIDUALS	Feed the correct amount according to the horse's weight, work, stabled/turnout, time of year, age, rider's ability, good doer/poor doer.	Maintain horse's weight, condition and ability to work.
QUALITY	Feed good quality fodder.	Poor quality feed is a false economy. The horse may need more or develop digestive or respiratory problems or may not eat.
HYGIENE	Use clean utensils.	Reduce the risk of infection and contamination and not put horse off food.
ROUTINE	Keep to the horse's feeding routine.	Changes in feeding routine can cause colic.
CHANGES	Make no sudden changes.	The gut needs to adapt slowly to changes in diet.
FIBRE	Plenty of fibre.	Keeps the gut healthy and slows digestion so that all food is digested and absorbed efficiently and keeps digestive system functioning.
LITTLE AND OFTEN	Feed little and often.	The horse has a small stomach and naturally grazes up to 20 hours per day. Feeding should mimic this.
EXERCISE	Allow 1 hour once the horse has eaten before exercising	The blood supply will be in the gut, aiding digestion and cannot be used for muscular work. A full stomach can restrict lung capacity by pressing on the diaphragm.
WATER	Clean fresh water should be available at all times.	Water is required by all systems in the body to function efficiently.

ANSWERS/12 WATERING AND FEEDING

Q12.6

	ADVANTAGE	DISADVANTAGE
STREAM	Constant supply.	Can become poached and the horse stuck. A sand bed can give the horse sand colic. You don't know if something is contaminating the water upstream.
FILLABLE TROUGH	Large static vessel. Can see if the horses are drinking.	Requires manual filling.
AUTOMATIC WATER TROUGH	Large vessel. Labour saving. Constant supply.	Unable to monitor the quantity being drunk.
BUCKETS	Ability to monitor the quantity of water being drunk.	Labour intensive. Small, therefore need many, and strong possibility of getting knocked over.
WATER BUTTS	Ability to monitor the quantity of water being drunk.	Labour intensive. Preferable to buckets as they are larger and therefore less likely to be knocked over.

Q12.7

- Using tie-rings on the fencing, tie the herd up and feed each individually.
- If all horses in the herd have the same feed, space buckets out evenly, with one or two extra put out to prevent bullying. Remove a known bully and feed him by himself.

Q12.8

Hay
Haylage
Succulents
High fibre cubes
Alfalfa
Chaff
Sugar beet

Q12.9

PELLETS — 24 hours
SHREDS — 12 hours
SPEEDIBEET — 15 minutes
Always check and follow the instructions on the bag.

Q12.10

A Fill and weight the haynet.
B Put in bin and fully immerse with water.
C Drain after allotted time.
D Tie haynet correctly in the stable.

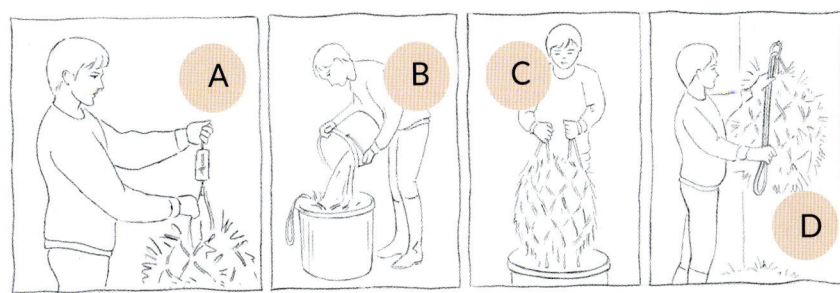

Q12.11

Swells the hay seeds so that they are digested, not inhaled.
Washes spores away so that they are not inhaled.
Prevents horses coughing.
Removes nutrients from the hay for overweight horses.

13 GENERAL KNOWLEDGE

Q13.1

Safeguarding	Every yard should have a person who has undergone safeguarding training. If you have any concerns about children or vulnerable adults these should be reported to the designated person.
Health and safety	Take reasonable care of your own and others safety, including following instructions from your employer or supervisor, wearing suitable personal protective equipment (PPE) and reporting any safety concerns to a senior staff member.
Equality and diversity	Treat all colleagues and clients with respect. If you feel anyone is being discriminated against report this to a senior staff member.
Data protection	Staff and client personal information must be kept confidential.
Animal welfare concerns	Report any concerns to a senior member of staff.

Q13.2

Jodhpurs. Sturdy boots. Long sleeved top. Waterproof coat. Comfortable, well fitting trousers.

Q13.3

- Bin — therefore no litter on yard.
- 'No smoking' signs.
- Fire extinguishers.
- Fire drill notice with 999 Fire Brigade number and meeting point.
- Using circuit breaker.
- Alarm.

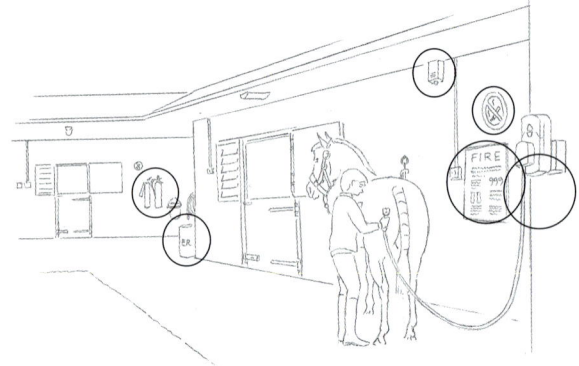

Q13.4

Assess the situation.
Prevent further accidents.
Assess the casualty.
Call for help.

14 RIDING

Q14.1

- If others are already in the school, ask permission to enter.
- Keep a safe distance from other horses at all times.
- Be aware of other riders at all times.
- If riding in open order, pass left hand to left hand, when at the same pace.
- Give faster paces the right of way on the outer track.
- If a rider is having problems, keep out of their way.
- If others are still riding as you leave, ask permission before exiting.

Q14.2

1. Rider and leader wearing hat, gloves and correct footwear and are carrying short whips.
2. Horse being led from the right side, with whip in right hand.
3. Half a horse's length between both horses.

4. Rider is thanking driver for slowing down.
5. The ridden horse's tack looks to be in good condition.
6. The led horse has his stirrups run up and secured to prevent them from sliding down and spooking the horse.
7. The horse is led in a bridle.
8. Horses are correctly shod.
9. Riders are wearing high visibility clothing.
10. Horses are wearing high visibility clothing.

Q14.3

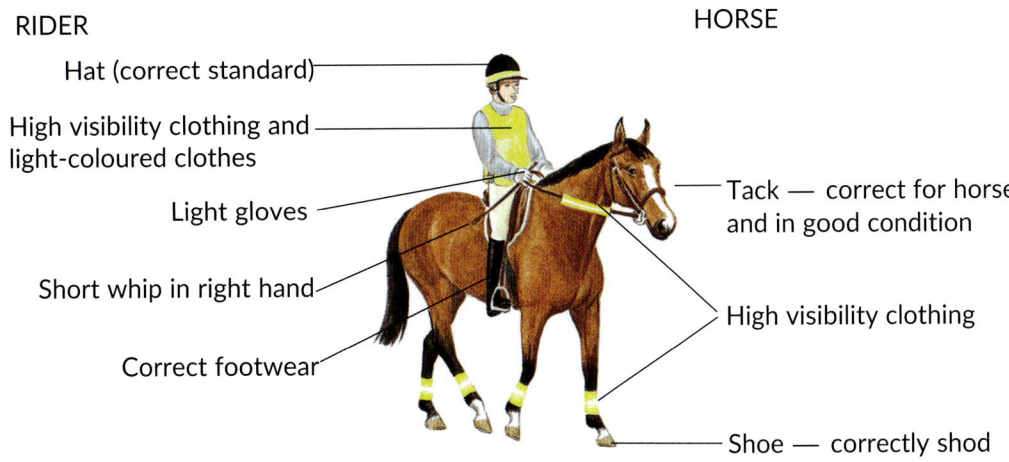

Q14.4

Observe, signal, observe, manoeuvre.

Q14.5

1. Observe, signal
2. Halt; look right, left, right; look behind right and if the situation has changed at all, signal again before manoeuvre.
3. Walk a straight line to the other side of the road and turn right (looking both ways as you cross the road).
4. Look in front and behind to assess new surroundings and hazards.

Q14.6

1. Observe, signal
2. Observe behind right, lifesaver look left and turn left, if safe.
3. Look down the new road for any hazards.
4. Look in front and behind.

Q14.7

RIDER — Hat silk. Jacket. Tabard. Gloves.
HORSE — Bridle. Reins. Breastplate. Leg wraps. Exercise sheet. Saddle cover. Stirrup tabs.

Q14.8

Walk when passing other horses.
Leave gates as found.
Observe the Country Code.
Pass left to left in single file.

Q14.9

CORRECT

1. In trot. The horse wears a running martingale. The reins remain threaded through the martingale and are therefore not taken over the head. The handler runs on the left side, by the horse's shoulder, with only the right hand holding the reins under the horse's chin. Whip in left hand.
5. Walk by shoulder, left side, reins over head, held in two hands, whip in left hand. Horse and rider looking straight ahead.

INCORRECT

2. Leading in front of the horse.
3. Walking without awareness for horse, and horse not straight or concentrating.
4. Running martingale attached, reins taken over the head to lead.
6. Dragging the horse.

Q14.10

- Shoes – secure.
- Correct tack.
- Stitching of tack is in good order.
- Girth is attached to girth straps 1 and 2 or 1 and 3.
- Numnah loops are attached to girth straps and girth.
- Latches on stirrups bars are down.
- Girth is tightened to mount.

Q14.11

Measure stirrup length along the underside of your arm.

Q14.12

A Place the reins over the horse's head.
B Tighten the girth, ensuring that the numnah is pulled up into the gullet of the saddle.
C Estimate the correct length of the stirrups by positioning the leather under the arm.

ANSWERS/14 RIDING

either

D Mounting block. Lead the horse to the mounting block and take up the contact. Place left foot in left stirrup and lightly swing right leg over, landing gently in the saddle.

or

E Mount from the ground. Take up the contact, face horse's tail, position left foot in left stirrup, reach for the waist of the saddle on the offside, and bounce lightly up to gently sit in the saddle.

or

F Receive a leg-up. Take up the contact, bend the left leg at the knee, discuss with the person giving the leg-up on which count to jump, jump high and lightly sit in the saddle.

G Place both feet in stirrups. In a safe area, check girth and tighten if necessary.

H Adjust stirrups as necessary, using one hand, keeping the feet in the stirrups as they are adjusted.

Q14.13

CORRECT— (A) Stirrup on the ball of the foot, turned from the front to the outside so that the leather lies flat along the lower leg.

INCORRECT — (B) Stirrup leather twisted the wrong way.
(C) Peacock safety stirrup with the elastic on the inside.
(D) Adult safety stirrup (bent iron) with the curve on the outside.

Q14.14

SIDE

Cavesson noseband fastened on the outside of the cheekpiece.
Bit too low in mouth.
Browband over ear.
Throatlash too tight.
Saddle too far back.
Stirrups too long.
Numnah slipped back under the saddle.

BEHIND

Saddle hanging to one side.
Stirrups unlevel.
Numnah not symmetrical over the horse's back.

Q14.15

Thumb on top of the reins

Little finger under the reins

Hands held about 4–6ins (10–15cm) apart, with thumbs on top

Q14.16

GOOD	BAD
Head up.	Head down.
Shoulders straight.	Shoulders rounded.
Back straight.	Back rounded.
Arms bent at the elbow.	Arms straight.
Hands held correctly.	Hands low.
Hips straight.	Hips rolled back too far.
Soft knee with a gentle bend.	Knee too far forward.
Lower leg underneath the rider.	Lower leg too far forward.
Heel directly under hip.	Heel too far forward.
Toes forward.	Toes pointing outward.

Q14.17

Having changed the rein and balanced the horse, place both reins into the outside hand. Using the inside hand, pull the whip through to the inside. Replace one rein in each hand. Position the whip correctly over the knee.

Q14.18

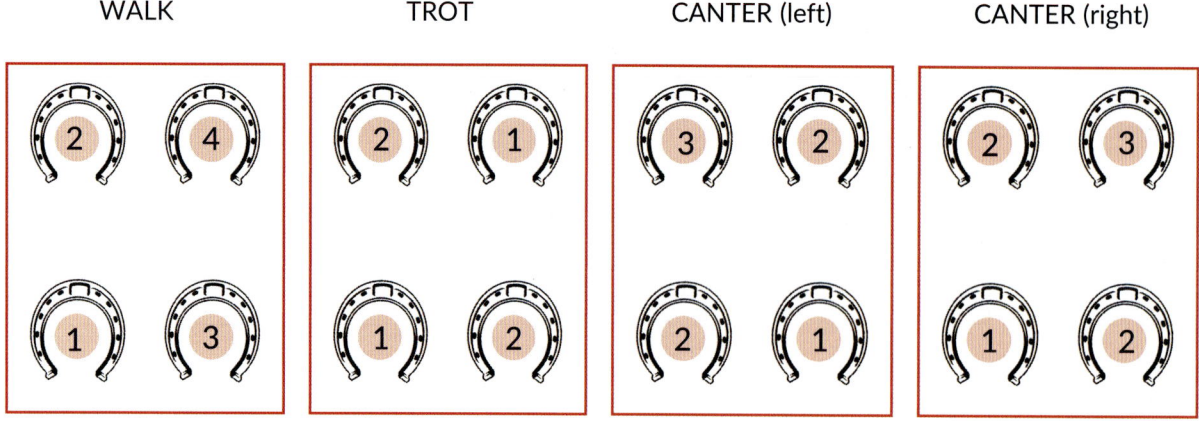

Q14.19

Maintain a rhythm.
Forwards enough so the rest of the ride do not need to slow down.
Not so forwards that the rest of the ride are left behind.
Listen to instructions.
Follow instructions accurately.
Ride accurate school figures.

Q14.20

Remove both feet from the stirrups. Pull the right buckle away from the stirrup bar. Cross the stirrup and leather over to lie neatly on the horse's left shoulder, in front of the saddle. Repeat with the left side.

Q14.21

HEAD	Looking ahead.
SHOULDERS	Square and straight.
BACK	Straight.
HIPS	Out of saddle, soft joints.
KNEES	Lying on the saddle, soft joints.
LOWER LEG	Against the horse's side — security.
ANKLES	Soft joints.
HEELS	Down — security and balance.

Q14.22

LEGS — light squeeze with the inner calf.
SEAT AND BODY — even, light weight over both seat bones. Upper body tall. Shoulders directly above hips.
HANDS — still, level contact used in a take-and-release movement.
VOICE — usually only used when lungeing or bringing on a young horse. Penalised if used in dressage competition.
WHIP — used to reinforce the leg aid if required.

ANSWERS/14 RIDING

Q14.23

When riding on the left rein, the rider should be on the left trot diagonal. This can be recognised by looking at the horse's outside (right) shoulder, and with more experience, the rider will be able to feel whether they are right or wrong. When looking at the outside shoulder, the rider should be sitting as the shoulder moves back, and rising as it travels forwards. Being on the correct diagonal helps the horse's balance and the co-ordination of the rider's aids.

Q14.24

1 Short diagonal
2 Long diagonal
3 Centre line
4 B – E
5 Two half 20m circles, A – X, X – C
6 Two half 10m circles, E – X, X – B
7 Half 15m circle, inclining back to the track
8 Half 10m circle, inclining back to the track
9 Four-loop serpentine

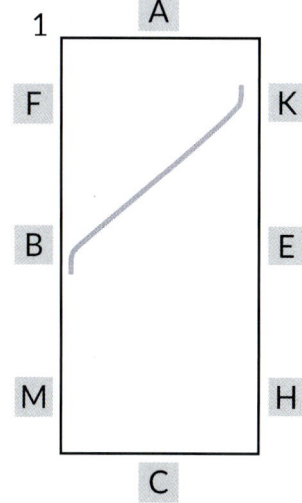
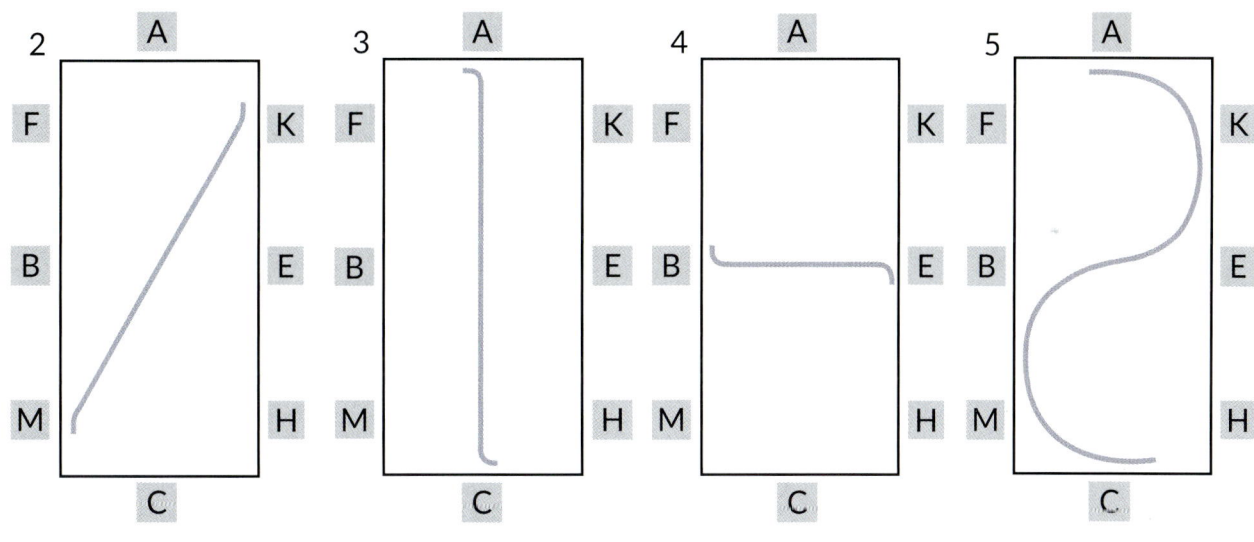
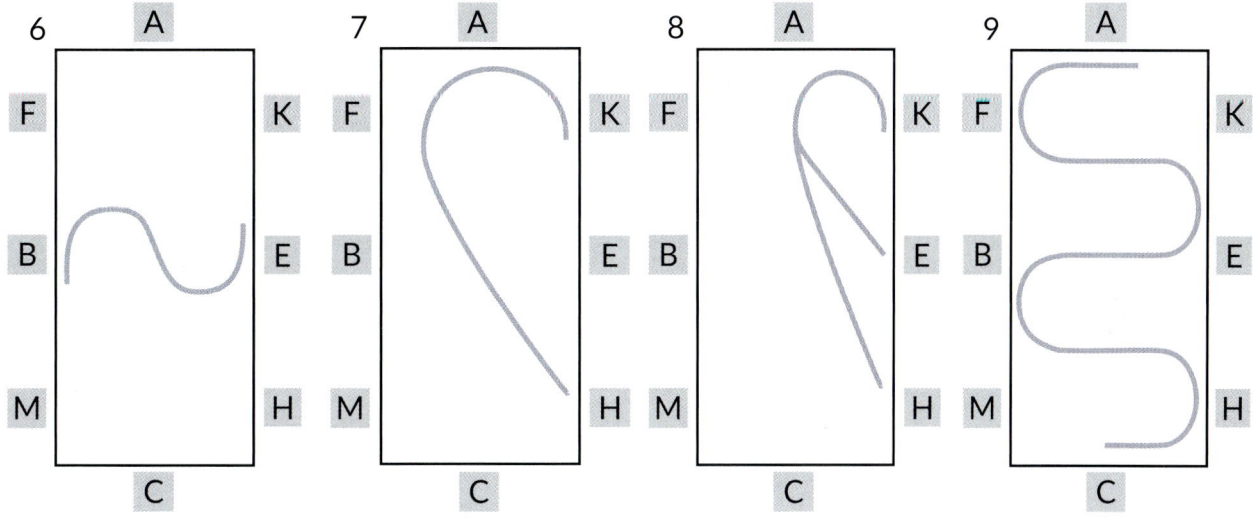

FURTHER READING

The following books can all be obtained from the BHS Bookshop.

  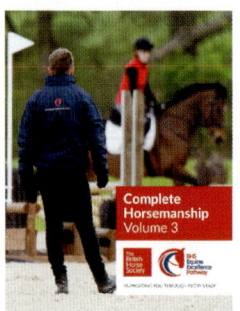 

  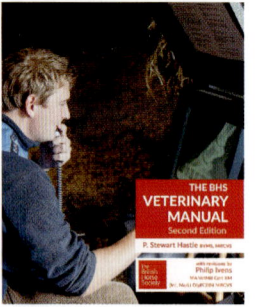  

USEFUL ADDRESSES

The British Horse Society
Equestrian House
Abbey Park
Stareton
Kenilworth
Warwickshire
CV8 2XZ
tel: 02476 840500
website: www.bhs.org.uk
email: enquiry@bhs.org.uk

BHS Equine Excellence Team
tel: 02476 840508
email: pathways@bhs.org.uk

BHS Approvals Department
tel: 02476 840509
email: approvals@bhs.org.uk

BHS Bookshop
tel: 02476 840513
website: www.britishhorse.com